HOW TO BE A
GOVERNMENT
WHIP

HOW TO BE A
GOVERNMENT
WHIP

Helen Jones

Biteback Publishing

First published in Great Britain in 2016 by
Biteback Publishing Ltd
Westminster Tower
3 Albert Embankment
London SE1 7SP
Copyright © Helen Jones 2016

ISBN 978-1-78590-062-4

10 9 8 7 6 5 4 3 2 1

A CIP catalogue record for this book is available from the British Library.

Set in Quadraat by Adrian McLaughlin

Printed and bound in Great Britain by
CPI Group (UK) Ltd, Croydon CR0 4YY

MIX
Paper from
responsible sources
FSC® C020471

Contents

Chapter 1

Appointment

'YOU'RE VERY POPULAR in the PLP,' Gordon Brown told me when he rang to confirm my appointment as a whip.

I sighed and thought, 'Well, you've just put an end to that.'

The first thing to remember if you wish to be a whip is that you are not entering a popularity contest. In fact, becoming a whip means an end to popularity altogether. From now on, you will, like it or not, be a person your colleagues love to hate. You will need superhuman reserves of stamina, guile and even charm as you seek to keep the government on the road but all you will receive in return is the deep suspicion of your colleagues, who will retain the ingrained belief that you are lying to them whenever you speak. You should not take this personally. Much of the time it will probably be true.

The first problem you will have to deal with is the decision of whether or not to accept the job offered to you. It might seem obvious that you will. Most MPs do because they are delighted to be asked to be part of the government, even if it is only on the bottom rung. Still, you should remember that being a whip is different from any other ministerial post. For one thing, it does not give you a public profile. You will not be able to delight the House with your dazzling displays of oratory, and any visions you have of sharing your thoughts with a grateful public via the Today programme should immediately vanish from your mind. Whips should never give interviews and, from now on, your public utterances will be limited to 'I beg to move that this House do now adjourn' or, when asked when a particular piece of legislation is to be taken, 'Tomorrow'. (Now and again, to bring a little variety into your dull life, you will be asked to respond to the same question by saying 'Monday next'.) None of these interventions in parliamentary life will get you into the headlines.

In fact, you will lose the right to express an opinion on anything, except within the confines of the Whips' Office (where you will hear opinions on every issue, as well as on both the parentage of a number of ministers and their competence expressed loudly and clearly). Instead, you will learn to tell your colleagues about the huge value of a piece of legislation while personally believing it to be dangerous or useless, and you will do so with a smile. If in government, you will become one of 'the Prime Minister's whips', and your duty will be to get the legislation *they* want through Parliament. You will learn the mantra of the Whips' Office, as expressed pithily by Nick Brown, a former Chief Whip: 'We don't do policy, we do process.' Unless you can not only accept all this, but learn to enjoy it, you should not even think of entering the Whips' Office.

Of course, some people do not heed this advice because they see being a whip as the route to a successful career in government. Their wish is seldom granted, however, because they invariably make bad whips. There are a number of Prime Ministers who thought the same way, seeing a stint in the Whips' Office as a useful grounding for future ministers. There are others who ignore it completely until forced to contemplate making appointments, who never realise that a good Whips' Office is a vital component of successful government. It is a good idea, therefore, if you think you may be offered the job of whip, to consider carefully beforehand whether it is really the right one for you. Of course, this is only possible if you are not taken by surprise, if you have some inkling that you are under consideration in the first place. People often do know when their names are in the frame, but that is not to say that they will be successful. Other poor souls delude themselves in every reshuffle that their time has come, only to find that, to their consternation, they have been unaccountably passed over yet again. Such sad individuals prove the truth of what Diane Abbott once told me when she said that 'the only place to be in a reshuffle is to know that you are either definitely getting a job or that you definitely aren't'. Anything else is torture. If you are not in one of these fortunate categories, think through your options beforehand so that you know what you could accept and what you couldn't. Better a happy backbencher than a miserable whip.

Up until my appointment in 2008, I had spent most of my career in Parliament knowing that I definitely *wouldn't* get a job, so the agony of reshuffles had passed me by. This time was different, however, and I learnt what many had before me: that the last people to be appointed in a reshuffle are the junior whips. At the time I was appointed, the Prime Minister Gordon Brown went to France part-way through the changes in the government and attended to international affairs, apparently with little thought of the torment he was inflicting on those waiting for his decision. Even without this added delay and complication in my case, the process is invariably awful. Your friends in Parliament may have already received the call and will telephone you to boast (very self-effacingly) of their appointment as Parliamentary Under-Secretary for Drains. They will try to feign concern because you have heard nothing, even though they are really too excited by their own sudden elevation to care. Remember to stay calm. Their elation will fade when they discover that the life of a junior minister is nasty, brutish and short. They will get all the late-night Adjournment Debates, all the policy areas the more senior ministers don't care about, and all the visits and conferences no one else wants to do because they are so boring. They will also get boxes of papers to take home every night and at weekends. You, on the other hand, will decide whether they get time off.

If you become a whip you will, like them, also work long hours (some of them hours of indescribable tedium), but you will have colleagues and the banter of a communal office to support and sustain you. Red boxes will be replaced by late-night phone calls when there is a panic on, making desperate attempts to track down wandering MPs, who are often on the other side of the world. You will never be off-duty and you will be the recipient of your colleagues' anxieties and complaints. If you cannot do all this and maintain a sense of humour, then you really should not become a whip.

Whatever the view of the current Prime Minister, the truth is that there are always two types of people who can work in the Whips' Office in government. The first group are those who see it as a preparation for what they consider better things, the 'ministers-in-training'. They might be perfectly good whips, and they can become better ministers for learning how the House of Commons works, but they are looking to move on. Others are the born whips. They love working behind the scenes, they like the adrenalin rush of close votes, and they enjoy the fun that comes from working in a communal office, rather than being stuck away somewhere on their own as a lonely junior minister. From time to time, these people get transferred elsewhere but, even if they become competent ministers, their hearts are not in it and, when they are back in the House, they return to the Whips' Office like wandering spirits seeking their true home. They are usually welcome, unless the personnel in the office has been completely changed, as there is an unspoken fraternity of whips, the neglected toilers in the engine room of Parliament.

If you are going to be appointed to the Whips' Office, you will receive a call from the Chief Whip before the Prime Minister speaks to you. The Chief gets a lot of say in who is appointed to the office, so the fact that he or she is calling you means that he probably wants you there (although any Chief Whip will have to accept some appointments he doesn't want as part of the process of negotiations). Be thankful and enthusiastic, but don't go over the top. Anyone who becomes Chief Whip will have heard it all before and, by this stage in the reshuffle, he will be tired and contemplating the vast amount of work waiting for him bedding in a new team, especially if he has just moved to the job himself. Your best approach is to make clear that you're looking forward to it and that you will take on any job he asks you to do. Don't start telling him you want a particular department to look after: life in the Whips' Office doesn't work that way and he will mark you down as another problem he has to deal with rather than someone who will take trouble away from him.

Later, and it may be much later, you will receive a call from the Prime Minister who, remember, is ringing you as a courtesy and not because he has a bit of spare time to fill. Learn from my experience – it's sensible to stay at home if you can until you have received the call. I set off for London in a burst of enthusiasm, wanting to be ready to start my new job early the next day. As a result, I got stuck in a motorway tail-back while Gordon Brown was trying to ring me and couldn't get off the road to take the call from Downing Street. When I finally managed to do this, I found an exasperated message on my mobile from Tom Watson, telling me that the Prime Minister had been trying to ring me for half an hour. I therefore began my stint in government by apologising profusely to the man who was trying to appoint me. My only defence was that the alternative was to start by being fined for using my mobile while driving. Neither of these is a great idea, so wait by the phone for the call.

Assuming you have decided that the Whips' Office is the place for you and have accepted the job, or even if you have been dragooned into it unwillingly, your first task will be to deal with the reactions of your colleagues. These will vary according to who you are dealing with. Your real friends will be genuinely pleased for you. They will send you cards and texts congratulating you and they will mean it. Others will pretend to be pleased for you while believing that they could do the job as well, or better, than you. You should remember that they may well be right. In any reshuffle, there are people who miss out on appointments and promotions for various reasons that have nothing to do with their ability. Maybe they didn't have anyone of influence putting their case, or they were in line for a job and lost out simply because there weren't enough to go round. They could simply be people of ability who are just not obsequious enough. You should bear with them, as they are struggling with disappointment and doing their best to hide it.

Others, on the other hand, will be grumpy and show it. When I was appointed, I was told by one Labour MP that 'there will be trouble with this Whips' Office'. He was disgruntled because a number of the appointees had been rebels at one time or another. He had been led to believe by a previous Chief Whip that, by swallowing his doubts and being mind-numbingly loyal, while keeping her informed about what his colleagues were up to, he would, one day, be rewarded with promotion. He wasn't, not only because he did not have the right personality to be a whip, but because nobody likes a snitch. Shrug your shoulders when faced with someone like this and remind yourself that there is a difference between being loyal and being a creep. As a whip, you should never trust someone in the latter group.

In my case, my appointment was also greeted with incredulity by many people. When Fabian Hamilton, an old friend from Leeds, first saw me standing by the tellers' desks during a vote (whips stand there to tell colleagues how many votes they can expect), he collapsed into genuine laughter. 'Oh my God! You're a whip!' he managed to gasp when he'd got his breath. The reason was simple: I had waited eleven years to become a promising newcomer and not only had I voted against the government on two pieces of legislation, I was well known both for having opinions and for expressing them. Tony Blair, who wasn't good at dealing with stroppy northern women, if he ever realised that I existed, had found this enough to keep me on the back benches: Gordon Brown was obviously either more forgiving or more desperate. Yet, Fabian's laughter, and that of some of my other colleagues, was not ill-natured. They were pleased that one of the 'excluded' had finally made it and my promotion, such as it was, meant that there was hope for us all.

Whatever reaction you receive from your colleagues, you should never lose sight of one important fact: everyone returns to the back benches eventually, and all government jobs should be regarded as temporary. Modesty on appointment and graciousness when sacked should be your rule, and the old truism about being nice to people on the way up because you meet them again on the way down should be constantly in your mind. The reason it's a truism is because it's true. So, however pleased you are, and however much you think you deserve your promotion, you should never celebrate openly. Some people have lost their jobs to make way for you and it is unwise to rub their noses in it. Other colleagues will simply think that you are crass. One group of new ministerial appointees in the 2001 parliament forgot this and congregated noisily in the Members' dining room, where they downed bottles of champagne with their meal. This simply served to earn them the loathing of many of their colleagues, especially those who had been in Parliament longer. As, one by one, they lost their jobs and, in some cases, their seats, no one who had watched them that night felt a pang of regret. Allow yourself a modest celebration with your family if you wish to, but other MPs will appreciate it more if you just get quietly on with your job. Enjoy it while it lasts, but don't ever believe your position is permanent.

You will also receive a salary, unless you are one of those people who accepts a job as an unpaid minister. If you are offered an unpaid post, you should think carefully before accepting it as a labourer is worthy of his hire, and you will look so desperate to get your foot on the ladder of promotion that most of your colleagues will despise you for doing it. Prime Ministers have taken to using this device as a way of getting around the fact that only a certain number of paid ministerial posts are allowed. You do not have to join in the game.

The best advice about your salary is not to use it for every-day living expenses. It is a bonus and one you will not have for ever, so set up a system that ensures it goes straight out of your current account and into savings. Pay more off your mortgage, or save up for something special, but do not get used to living off it. If you do, you risk becoming one of those ex-ministers who find that they cannot live on a backbencher's salary. Since these are often the same people who have lectured their colleagues about why they cannot expect a pay rise, they are seldom popular. They become even less so when they are constantly seeking time off to serve the interests of Megacorp PLC while others carry the burden of hanging around for late votes to keep the government in office. More importantly, you will become a slave to the extra salary, desperate to hang on to your job, or any job, whatever you have to do. Not only will this make you a very poor whip, it will lose you a lot of friends. Sensible people will despise you and you will not be able to carry out one of the most important functions of the Whips' Office, which is to tell the Prime Minister things he doesn't want to hear when he needs to hear them.

Stay away from the temptation and keep repeating regu-larly to yourself that everyone gets sacked in the end. With this cheerful thought in mind, you can begin work.

Chapter 2

Know your office

GOVERNMENT WHIPS WORK from two offices in the House of Commons, one just off the Members' lobby and another just down the stairs. With one of the flights of imagination for which whips are famous, these are called the Upper Whips' Office and the Lower Whips' Office. You will need to decide which one you want to work in (and you should do this in advance as whips are ruthless in their scramble for desks). They are whips, after all.

If you are a Labour whip, the advantage of working down in the Lower Office is that you will not be directly under the all-seeing eye of the Deputy Chief Whip, who presides upstairs and who will rule much of your life from now on. Do not think you can avoid him altogether though. A good Deputy is always on the prowl and ever-alert for things going wrong. Being in the Upper Whips' Office will place you closer to the action, but gives you less opportunity to hide. Bear in mind that many of the desks will already be occupied by more senior whips and the old hands, so you will have to move quickly after your first meeting if you want to base yourself there.

That first meeting is likely to take place fifteen minutes before the day's business starts. Everyone – all the whips, the newly appointed and the old hands – will crowd into the Upper Whips' Office, perched on desks and sofas if they don't have their own desk there, to go through the business of the day. You may be expecting grandiose statements about how vital you are to the government or a rousing welcome from your colleagues. Forget it. You are now in a place where the business of the House is what matters; the forgotten, coal-shovelling engine room of Parliament and, just like engineers toiling in the bowels of a ship, whips are grafters. Grand gestures and sweeping statements are for others and done elsewhere.

You will also learn that the first rule of a whip's life is 'be punctual'. The meeting will start the moment the annunciator shows the right time, with no allowances made for latecomers. Anyone who arrives late or, God help them, is absent, will find themselves having to give an explanation to the Deputy Chief Whip or, more informally, to their colleagues. Take the rule to heart and never, ever miss the daily meeting unless you have got permission in advance. It will rarely be given. The death of a close relative is just about acceptable as an excuse, but it must be a parent or sibling. Your own illnesses will not count unless you are at death's door, otherwise you will be expected to struggle in and spread your germs around the office. The Deputy will see this as character building. It toughens you up so that you can refuse other people time off.

There is a good reason behind the emphasis on punctuality. You will learn quickly that, if you are not on time, a motion which should be moved may not be, something will go wrong in a committee you are supposed to be in charge of, or the opposition will take advantage of your absence and a vote may be lost. If the government's business does not go through and you are in charge at the time, you will have committed the whips' greatest sin. The discipline of rigidly enforced punctuality is designed to help avoid this, so get used to it. If you are not in the room before the door is shut and the 'meeting in progress' sign is put on the door, you will be marked down as unreliable.

Little time is allowed for discussion at these meetings: that will take place elsewhere. The Deputy simply runs through the business of the day, gets reports from the whip in charge of whatever Bill is being debated and goes through any problems. Then he will appoint tellers for the votes and whips to stand on the 'box', as the clerks' desks inside the lobbies are known. You will not, at this stage, understand much of what is going on. Just nod sagely as if everything is clear and do not try to start a debate on the content of the legislation. That is no longer your role.

It is usual for the Deputy to then hand over to the Chief Whip, who has his own office just behind the main Whips' Office. At my first meeting, when I heard the words, 'Colleagues, the Chief' and Nick Brown, the least pompous of men, stepped through from his office, I was tempted to burst into a chorus of 'Hail to the Chief'. If you find yourself similarly tempted, then it is wise to resist. You are now part of a world where what 'the Chief' says is law and you will soon find yourself constantly adopting the same mode of address, asking 'Is the Chief in?' and 'What does the Chief say?' as if they are the most normal questions in the world. In your world, they are.

After a few brief words of welcome to newcomers and congratulations to those who have stayed on or have been promoted, the meeting will end and 'grab a desk' time begins. This is when you need to take stock of your surroundings and of your new colleagues.

The Whips' Office is a living example of a contradiction. Almost everyone gets the same pay, everyone except the Chief Whip works in a large, communal, crowded office, yet the whole organisation works on a hierarchy. In a Labour Whips' Office there is an 'executive' or 'top table' of four people: the Chief Whip, his deputy, the third in line and the number four. For some historical reasons, which I never quite fathomed, all of these top four, except the Chief Whip, hold titles in the royal household: Comptroller of Her Majesty's Household, Treasurer of Her Majesty's Household and Vice-Chamberlain of Her Majesty's Household. At the time of my appointment, these posts were held by Tommy McAvoy, John Spellar and Claire Ward respectively. At the next reshuffle, I was to be appointed as the Vice-Chamberlain. Fortunately, no real duties in the household are involved, a fact for which the Queen is, no doubt, as thankful as the whips. From time to time, these people will all disappear into the Chief Whip's office for an urgent conference, as may the pairing whip, who, confusingly, may or may not also hold one of the top posts. You would be well advised not to enquire what they are discussing as you will simply look nosy. Get on with your own job and, when they trust you enough, they will tell you.

In my time, the office was presided over by Tommy McAvoy, one of the best whips the Labour Party has ever had, who sat at the top of the room next to John Spellar. On Tommy's desk, there was a piranha fish (dead but real) and a sign that said: 'Feminism spoken here.' The first was there to remind people never to offend the Deputy Chief Whip, and the second a rebuke to those who felt he wasn't 'family-friendly' enough. His choice of both objects is worth remembering. Many people have the mistaken impression that the Whips' Office is some kind of personnel department, there to assist people with their problems and to help them develop their careers. If you have entered the office with this idea in your head, you should get rid of it immediately. There will be times when whips recognise and help with personal problems, they may even talent-spot, but in my experience their views are seldom influential. These roles, however, are secondary to their main purpose in life, which is simply to get government legislation through the House. From the moment of your appointment, that is your job and everything else is comes second. Your colleagues may be ill, dealing with family problems, or be tired and depressed. As a human being, you will sympathise. You can, and will want to, help them. As a whip, you will want to get them into the lobby for a crunch vote by any means possible in order to ensure the survival of the government. Do not fool yourself into believing you are there for any other reason. Your colleagues will be glad of your sympathy, but the government would rather have their votes.

As you settle in, you will discover that others hold various titles too. Some whips, who have been in the office a while, are Lords Commissioners of Her Majesty's Treasury and are allowed to sign important documents. You may rather like the idea of this until you discover that, during a crisis, they are roused in the middle of the night and dragged to the Treasury.

The rest of the people in the office are simply 'whips' or 'assistant whips', and you will have joined with the lowly rank of the latter. The title may fool you into believing that you will learn your job as some kind of apprentice, by helping out someone more experienced than you. Unfortunately, this is not true and you will be thrown in at the deep end but, as whips, you will be told to 'help each other'. This is, as always, more true of some people than others. What you need is an old hand who doesn't feel threatened by the arrival of new people and who will show you the ropes. Find that person straight away or you will be floundering for weeks. Ask if you can sit with them on the bench and watch what they do, and then get them to explain anything you don't understand. You may think that you know all about how the House of Commons works, but you have seen it only as a backbencher, not from the point of view of those who have to ensure that the business runs smoothly. Very soon, you will find yourself sitting on the front bench (and there is always a government whip there when the House is sitting), keeping an eye on what is happening and having to deal with any opposition attempts to disrupt things. It is wise to ensure that you know what you are doing *before* that happens.

The other group of people you need to know are the civil servants, who work in the back office. Some you will find in a cubbyhole behind the Upper Whips' Office; others are downstairs behind the Lower Whips' Office. All of them work long hours, help to manage crises and are underappreciated. Make them your friends and you will find that they are among the best of the civil service. They come to work in the Whips' Office because they want to and, not surprisingly, they have a much better understanding of Parliament and how it works than most civil servants you will encounter, who tend to see it as an institution that impedes the smooth running of government. They can give you valuable information and advice, and you will have many opportunities to be grateful to them during your time as a whip.

These are also the people who will bring you the forms you have to fill in, registering your home and London addresses and all your contact numbers. Do not even think of hiding any of these as whips are never off-duty and, from now on, you need to be contactable twenty-four hours a day, every day, wherever you are. From now on, you will not, ever, switch your mobile phone off. I have been contacted while sitting on the harbour at Dubrovnik, while walking on Lindisfarne, and when dropping off to sleep at 11.30 p.m. None of these calls were pointless or trivial. You will also find out from the civil servants what the perks of the job are. These are not many, so curb your excitement. You will have access to the government car pool and to the taxi firms with which the office has contracts. You may be lucky enough to live near the House and think you will never need a car, but you will change your mind after you have done a fourteen-hour day, most of which has been spent on your feet chasing votes. You will be even more grateful when you have to come into work even though you are ill. At that point, you will cease thinking of the cars as luxury and regard them as essential to keep you going. You can salve your conscience by giving lifts to other MPs who are not so fortunate, but who will also have had a long day. This will probably mean it would be quicker for you to walk home, if only your legs could manage it, but your colleagues will be grateful to you. Not offering lifts to them is a very bad habit for any minister to get into and you can be certain that they will hold it against you.

You will also be asked how you want your name to appear on your ministerial box. Fill in the form and, about six months later, when you have forgotten all about it, you will be pleasantly surprised by its arrival. You will have no use for it at all, since you do not have ministerial papers to take home and, if you are a good whip, you will never write down confidential information. Still, it will prove to your grandchildren that you were once a member of the government and, as it is lead-lined, you will be able to store your insurance policies in it in the meantime. It's nice to know that being a whip safeguards your policy in the event of a fire.

Chapter 3

How to cope with
your colleagues

I T IS A commonly held view that, to get their desired
outcome, all whips have to do is threaten people. However, like most commonly held views, this is a complete
fallacy. It would be very unwise to go into the Whips'
Office expecting to spend your time warning people of the dark
details of their personal lives that will appear in the papers
should they fail to vote with the government. In the first place,
you are unlikely to know such details until, like everyone else,
you read them in the *Mail* or *The Sun* when, like others in the
tea room, you will shake your head and say, 'You wouldn't have

thought he had it in him.' If someone is in trouble in their personal life, has left his wife for a nineteen-year-old topless model or decided, after thirty years of impeccable respectability and conformity, to throw it all away for a shack by a beach with a young man they met last week, the last person they will tell is a government whip. This is because they believe that you would use it against them – and they are probably right.

Secondly, you can only ever use such a threat once. If you do so, and the expected retribution does not materialise, no one will believe you ever again. In fact, it will almost *never* materialise because a good whip does not want bad publicity for the party. So threats should only ever be used as your last resort and then only against people who are threatening to vote against the government simply to make mischief, rather than for reasons of conscience or because of a deeply held and genuine belief that the government is wrong. If you try to threaten such people, then they will see themselves as martyrs for a cause and will only become even further entrenched in their position. They will never change their minds because it will look as if they're giving in to threats, as they will be. You should also bear in mind that they might actually be right in their view of a particular piece of legislation. After all, although you will never be able to admit it outside the safe haven of the Whips' Office, it has been known for governments to be wrong.

Former ministers should be treated with particular caution if they have served in the department that is now trying to put controversial legislation through. They may well have seen it proposed when they were in office and rejected it because they saw the problems. Just because the civil servants have now convinced a more compliant minister does not mean that the potential pitfalls have gone away and these ministers will know more about them than you. Don't try to argue with them. Just appealing to their loyalty works better because decent people don't want to cause problems for their successors.

However, if you wish to establish a reputation for being 'hard', you will be relieved to know that there is one group of people that you can threaten whenever you wish. These are former ministers who walked out of government just to cause trouble. They may have gone because they wished to unseat the Prime Minister or because they didn't get the job they wanted, or flounced out in a dispute about policy, but the one thing they will have in common is that they tried to damage their own party. These people will be fêted by the press, who love the good stories they have generated for them, but generally loathed by members of the party, who hate disloyalty above all else. They are likely to be in trouble with their own constituency parties and with their parliamentary colleagues, too, who believe that they have made life more difficult for everyone. These ex-ministers are usually those who have had a good run in government on a decent salary, but have started to believe their own publicity about how 'essential' they are to the running of the country. To make matters worse, they are often the very people who have lectured other MPs on loyalty when they have expressed the least scintilla of doubt about any government proposal. They are in much more trouble than they think and can be dealt with robustly.[1]

The rest of the people you deal with should be treated with respect, bearing in mind that you will be returning to the back benches at some point. You will be given your own little group of MPs to look after and for whom you will be responsible, and this will be either a regional group or part of one. These are members of, what the office terms, your 'flock'. You are responsible for keeping in touch with them, listening to their woes and helping them when you can. Unless you do this and take the trouble to build a relationship with them, you cannot expect them to listen to you when you need their support for the government. There will be days when you think that your flock were put on earth just to make your life difficult, days when you want to shout at them to get through the bloody lobby and stop whingeing. Sometimes you will, no doubt, have days when you don't think that anyone you deal with is actually human, but they are, and if you treat people badly, they will react badly to you.

For this reason, a good whip should not expect to spend all their time in the Whips' Office or, indeed, talking solely to other whips. The tea room, the dining room and the bar are as much your places of work as the office is. Listen to what people tell you, and try to assist them if they have a genuine grievance. It will often be that they are not being given time

---

1   See Chapter 6

off when they request it or that ministers are refusing to visit their constituencies. MPs are delicate plants and do not flourish on neglect. They may well have a constituency problem and cannot get a meeting with a minister to try to resolve it. Get them one. Ministers who do not have any respect for their colleagues don't deserve yours. Above all, take them seriously, and listen to their fears about what the government is doing. You should be able to distinguish between the serial moaners and those who have a genuine point. Bear in mind always that good whips are a conduit through whom information flows to and from the government and its backbenchers. All this hanging about is not time wasted but, rather, time invested. You are out in what Nick Brown used to call 'the body of the kirk' when he sent his whips out to mingle with the Parliamentary Labour Party (PLP) with the simple instruction: 'Be whips.'

While you are engaged in this listening exercise, it is important to understand that the members of your flock, as with all the members of the parliamentary party, will usually fall into one of several categories. Understanding the difference between them is the key to knowing how to deal with people.

1. The serial rebels

These are the people who will vote against the government for any reason. They may have had two emails complaining about something, or there's an 'r' in the month, or it has rained for three days in a row. They really don't need an excuse. Some of them believe that every Labour government is a sell-out and that they are the only true guardian of the socialist flame. Others are frightened the moment they hear a complaint or receive one letter from an unhappy constituent and genuinely think that, if they respond to every special interest group and every grievance by voting against their own government, they will save their seats. They have failed to work out that the message 'the Labour government is crap, vote Labour' has never worked. The same rule applies to every party.

There is very little you can do about the first group of serial rebel, except keep on good terms with them so that they tell you what they are planning to do, although, on occasions where a real meltdown is threatened, you may be able to persuade them to abstain. Since they believe they are the pure in heart, it is unlikely that you will be able to persuade them to actually vote with their own party. There were Labour MPs in Parliament before 2010 who had voted against the government more times than David Cameron. People like that are clearly a lost cause.

The second group can be challenged. They generally have no real ideological objection to what's going on, but they are fearful souls. When they tell you they have had 'loads of emails', ask them exactly how many (the number is usually no more than a dozen). Then ask them how many of the people who are threatening 'never to vote for your party again' actually voted Labour in the past. It is surprising how many people get themselves elected to Parliament and then forget to make this simple check when contacted by unhappy voters. Then reassure them that lots of people agree with what the government is doing, but will not be writing to them about it. You are on safe ground here since very few people have ever contacted their MP to tell him or her that they were happy. If that doesn't work, ask them how many of the people writing to them write about almost every issue. Some people write to their MP every week about whatever is in the news. By definition, this makes them unrepresentative of the electorate as a whole.

Remember that these fearful people need reassurance and that it is your job to convince them that they will lose more votes by rebelling than by voting with the government. It may even be true. There will be some statistics out there that may boost your argument but, on the whole, rebels do not do better than loyalists when a general election comes.

2. The unquestioning loyalists

These people are very easy to deal with, even if you find them extremely boring. They always vote with the government. No scintilla of doubt about its motives or tiny questions about its actions ever enter their minds. Indeed, they seldom bother looking closely at legislation because their trust is absolute. These are people who would happily troop through the lobbies to introduce the slaughter of the first-born or the Gas Chambers (Miscellaneous Provisions) Bill if a minister told them it was necessary. What is more, they would deliver a speech praising the legislation if they were asked to ('There is much to be said in favour of the slaughter of the first-born and those who resist it are simply refusing to modernise.').

You can give these people planted questions to ask and hand out speeches to deliver, and they will do so with pride. They long ago gave up thinking for themselves and conceded power over their thought processes to the government. They are also the resident school snitches who will be eager to tell you which of their colleagues have been disloyal. Beware of taking anything they say too seriously, however, since anyone expressing even the mildest of doubt is a traitor in their eyes. When you ring them to check on their voting intentions, you should never suggest that they might even *contemplate* voting against the government or they will be grossly insulted. Instead, say that you know they can be relied upon but that you are just ringing to check that they don't have an important constituency engagement on that day (they invariably have lots of these as the little world they inhabit cannot get on without them).

Such people are used all the time by whips, despite the fact that they really shouldn't be allowed to legislate. Treat them with some caution, however, especially if you have ever voted against the government, because they always believe that they could do your job much better than you and that only absolute, unquestioning loyalists should ever be whips.

3. The loyalists

These are the people who are born and bred within your party. If you cut them open, you would find its name running through them like the letters in a stick of rock. They have never considered, even in their youth, supporting any other party. In fact, they hate other parties with a passion and, because politics is not a game to them, they seldom have friends on the other side. They're loyalists; their friends are loyalists and their families are loyalists.

This group of people may, from time to time, disagree with the government – they may even rebel – but you can always rely on them when times are tough. They will come to the chamber to support ministers in trouble, turn up for important votes even when they are ill, and be prepared to take on the opposition at a moment's notice.

You should cherish these people and listen carefully when they tell you that something is wrong because they have the party's interests at heart. When they rebel, you should never use the old whip's trick of telling them that the government is going to lose to persuade them to change their vote – unless, of course, it really is going to lose and the damage that would result is serious. If that is the case, you can rely on them to come to the rescue, but these are not people you should mess about.

On less momentous occasions, these MPs may well think that the government needs to learn a lesson. One of my friends, who was opposed to a particular policy, was once told by a Chief Whip that, if she persisted, the government would lose. 'But I want them to lose,' was her obvious reply. The reason she was voting against was that she believed that what was being proposed was not only wrong, but 'not Labour'. Of course, because it's your job you will have to try to persuade people away from such a course, but learn to distinguish between the times when loyalists believe that they are pushing their government back in the right direction by making it more pure and times when the government is in real peril. These are people who believe strongly that, for example, any Labour government is better than a Tory government and who do not want to see their party out of office. In times of genuine danger, an appeal to their loyalty is enough, but you should always take their concerns very seriously and ensure that ministers are taking them seriously too. Don't ever let a minister dismiss them or their concerns as unimportant. It really isn't in anyone's interests not to listen to people who have their party's interests at heart. These people are the backbone of the parliamentary party, so anyone who thinks that way is too stupid to be a minister. Unfortunately for you, there are always a number of ministers like that.

4. The careerists

This group usually consists of newly elected MPs who are waiting for their multiplicity of talents to be recognised, although it also includes some MPs who, though they've been around for some time waiting to hear the call, still hope it will come, one day. They are distinguished from the unquestioning loyalists, who will continue to support a government that ignores them, because they are absolutely convinced of the righteousness of those they serve (hence the characterisation of some Blair loyalists as 'more Blairite than Tony').

Careerists may well turn out to be true believers in the long run but, at the moment, they are concerned with their own advancement. For a whip, this has numerous advantages. You can persuade them to attend incredibly boring debates and to speak in them, or to serve on numerous committees purely on the grounds that it will be good for their careers. Of course, you will not be so crass as to tell them this directly, but a suggestion that the Prime Minister personally takes an interest in this particular Bill, or that a minister has requested their presence in the debate because of their expertise in the subject, is usually enough to set them winging their way to a committee room or the Chamber like a homing pigeon.

When trying to fill standing committees, you can use the same tactic, but it can also be useful to imply that you are aware of lots of people who want to be on this committee for a particular Bill but that, as a great favour, you are giving them first refusal. Older hands will know that this is entirely untrue, but it usually works with ambitious newcomers. One ex-minister still remembers that, just after his arrival in Parliament, he was told by a whip that he had 'a nice little Bill' that would be 'good experience' for him. He accepted eagerly and then found himself stuck on a committee that went on for six months. Be warned, however: you can only use this trick once. When Frank Roy was trying to find people to fill the Bill that would enable Crossrail to be built, he suggested that he should get a badge that said: 'Fuck off, Frank', as that was what most people said when he approached them, before he had even had a chance to open his mouth. I warned that he would only get new people to do it as everyone else knew how long it would take. That was mostly true. It was relatively late in the parliament and most people had begun to understand how long such a hybrid Bill (one that involves public and private interests) would take. You just have to hope if you are ever in his position that there are enough people who are desperate for a job and who will try any means of getting one.

In politics, as elsewhere, you will find that the problem in dealing with ardent careerists is that often people's estimation of their own talent bears little relation to the existence of it. Some of the people who are seeking promotion will be ambitious people who are good at what they do, but others will be people who make the whole House groan (especially their own side) whenever they rise to speak or ask a question. Everyone else knows they are likely to make a hash of it and waits, tensed for the ridiculous point, or the opening that allows the other side to land a knockout blow. Yet, the careerist never realises this. He or she is instead convinced of their ability to deal the killer punch to the opposition and that their words of wisdom will be lapped up by a grateful nation. You really do not want these people in any debate for which you are responsible, because their 'killer punch' often turns out to be a boomerang that ends up hitting your own front bench. Ministers will not thank you for them, so do not ever ask them to speak and if you see them in the chamber, it's wise to make it clear in advance that any interventions they may make are nothing to do with you. Disowning them in advance is the only way to protect yourself from a disgruntled minister's anger.

Instead, when you have to organise a debate, try to find support for ministers by cultivating the people who do have talent, both among the obvious careerists and among the people who are quietly and competently getting on with their job. Many of the latter group are often cleverer, but less pushy. Make both groups your friends, encourage them to speak, feed them with killer questions that no one else has got. They may have to serve on some boring committees and sit through some very trying debates, but that is the price they pay for the chance to hone their debating skills. Anyway, you're a whip – abandon your finer feeling and forget about the boredom you are subjecting them to. Just be glad that you got them there.

5. The plotters

These are the really disgruntled – the people who hate the current leadership of your party and the government and who will do anything to get rid of them. There are some in every parliament, usually unable to reconcile themselves to the fact that their own candidate lost out and convinced that, however well the party is doing, it would be doing much better with someone else in charge. Although their sense of being the guardians of the only true path is not related to what the opinion polls say, these people tend to keep quiet in the good times and mostly hang around on the fringes of whatever is going on. In bad times, however, you can rely on them to come out of the woodwork. Since you are one of the Prime Minister's whips, it is your job is to protect his or her back.

This is where your contacts with the parliamentary party and your time spent conversing in the tea room will pay dividends. Because they are convinced that they are the keepers of the true flame, the only people who can save your party from meltdown, plotters are seldom discreet. Sit and watch and you will see them come and go, huddled in corners with like-minded souls, or trying to convert others by flitting from one group of people to another, dripping poison. One former minister hardly ever set foot in the tea room, not having a great love for many of her colleagues, but when she did, it was obvious to everyone that something was going on. If you have established a relationship of trust with your colleagues, then they will let you know what is afoot, and who is saying what and to whom, not as a tale-teller but in normal conversation. They will do this only if they know that you are not a tale-teller yourself and that you will not quote them as the source of your information or assume that they are involved in anything dubious. They will only believe this if you have shown in the past that you can listen to their concerns and feed them back without naming them and making them look like troublemakers. No one wants to be thought of as a plotter if they are not, so merely passing on the information to you should not mean that they are treated as one of the guilty. Make sure that you remember that when you report back, as you will have to.

You may well find that you have other sources of information too. One group of disaffected ministers in the last government met for regular suppers outside Parliament. Stupidly, they had this regular engagement put into their ministerial diaries and the whips always knew when this was happening through a contact with one of their diary secretaries. This proves two things. Firstly, Prime Ministers are not always wrong when they decide someone is not bright enough for the first rank and, secondly, being nice to people on the lower rungs of the Whitehall ladder pays off in the long term, often in unexpected ways.

Whichever way you get information like this, you must tell the Chief Whip immediately. While you should never bother the Chief Whip with trivia, plots against the Prime Minister, however hopeless, do not come under that heading. He will probably already know about it if he's up to the job, but he will welcome any extra information you can give him and, as an added benefit, you will have shown that you know *your* job. The reason is simple: you are one of the Prime Minister's whips and your duty is to him. If you can't carry out that duty effectively, then you shouldn't be in the job.

6. *The parliamentarians*

These are people beloved by the press and media. They are sages; the wise men and women who will pontificate on every bit of procedure and tell you how to change it. They may have been elected on your party ticket, but they forgot about it as soon as they arrived in Westminster. They seldom visit their constituencies because they have far more important things to do and they are the conscience of the nation – or, at least, the bits of the nation who read *The Guardian* and *The Independent*.

These are not people who learn to use the procedures of the House for a genuine and useful purpose, such as getting a Private Member's Bill through or amending Bills to make changes in the law. They do not even use the procedures to pursue any worthy cause, to remedy or raise awareness of an injustice. No, no – that would have some purpose. These are the pure theoreticians, who see changes to procedures as ends in themselves rather than as means to an end. They believe that Parliament is impotent and that it is their mission in life to save it. It is no use asking them how they know that if they have never tried using the procedures that are already in place. They will only look at you with astonishment – after all, in their minds they have far more useful work to do, such as write books and give interviews about the decline of democracy. Everyone loves them except their colleagues, who believe they are pompous twats, and their constituents, who are neglected in favour of their academic pursuits.

You cannot slap them down because they will run to the press and say you are trying to stifle democracy. You cannot appeal to their party loyalty because they devote most of their time trying to take the politics out of politics.

The only useful thing you can do with them is find them a committee engaged in investigating some abstruse constitutional matter. A review of the rules governing the procedures for private Bills or the powers of select committees are useful tools. House of Lords reform is not recommended, since it tends rouse too many passions and will be debated for ever when they produce their report without ever coming to a conclusion. It also gives the 'parliamentarians' too many opportunities to appear on TV and write columns in the newspapers.

Keep them occupied and then wait. Usually, they either lose their seats or step down and then you get to watch while they hand over to some poor unfortunate sap who is trying to make up for their years of neglect of the voters, without success. Such sages seldom do proper politics well and constituents don't read their books.

7. People with a conscience

Contrary to what most people outside think, there are a lot of such people in Parliament. They are not usually serial rebels, and certainly not unquestioning loyalists, but they may be good party members. They are loyal, but there are some issues on which they feel very strongly and will not budge. You should respect such people, for they remind you that you ought to listen to your conscience as well. Even if you parked it outside the door of the Whips' Office, you will need it back eventually.

Some issues are always regarded as conscience votes in Parliament, so Bills relating to abortion, the death penalty and so on are never whipped. Such votes are straightforward as far as you are concerned and you should never get involved with them, even if feelings are running high. Sometimes, one side or the other may well ask you to act as an unofficial whip for their cause. Never, ever accept, even if you believe in what they are trying to do. A 'free vote' will never be seen as such if anyone from the Whips' Office is involved and you will be accused of double-dealing by the other side. Stay out of it.

There are people who will want these issues whipped and, usually, they will tell you that the party has a policy on certain issues and it must be enforced on everyone. This is generally the case with any vote on abortion, where there are always people who simply refuse to accept that some of their colleagues have strong religious/moral beliefs on the issue. The best way to deal with these people is to remind them that the party has policies on lots of things and focus on something that you know they disagree with. Then ask them whether they would like the whip enforced on that. Your second line of defence is to point out that putting the whip on is a pointless exercise since it will not change anyone's vote and would simply lead to resignations from the front bench and the need to take disciplinary action against good colleagues. They don't usually care about this, but you should. It is not the job of the Whips' Office to create martyrs and some votes are just unwhippable. A good whip recognises the limits of what can be done.

Life gets more complicated when you are faced with a Bill that is more complex, because it deals with issues on which some people have strong conscientious, and often religious views, but which the government has taken a decision to support. The Human Fertilisation and Embryology Bill fell into this category, especially when attempts were made to amend it to deal with issues relating to abortion. The government was keen to see it pass into law, but not only could the clauses on abortion not be whipped, there were some people who had deeply held religious objections to certain parts of the original Bill. In such a case, it is usual to respect their views and give people a clear indication that their vote will not be held against them. A good whip knows that there are many things people will do for their party, but they will not change their religion or sense of morality for it. Do not let these people be dragged in to see ministers to be 'persuaded' of the error of their ways – it won't work and you will just be making life hard for decent people.

If anyone attempts to amend a Bill in a way that may make it a matter of conscience, then the Whips' Office may need to act. Attempts were made with the Human Fertilisation and Embryology Bill first to tighten the law on abortion, and then to liberalise it. The attempts to restrict access to abortion were never likely to pass and, therefore, did not concern the whips at the time, but when the Bill returned for its Report Stage, amendments were tabled which would have liberalised the law. The Chief Whip at the time was sympathetic, and argued that the government should make time available for these proposals to be debated, either during the passage of the Bill or at some future date. This was never going to happen. All governments want issues like abortion to be dealt with through Private Members' Bills, because they know that the legislation will split their own party and that it cannot be whipped.

Fortunately, the new Chief Whip realised what his predecessor had found so hard to grasp. If the amendments passed, the Bill would become an Abortion Bill and it therefore could not then be whipped at Third Reading. There was then a real possibility that the opposition, together with those who had objections to other parts of the Bill and those who could not vote for it on grounds of conscience, would combine to defeat it. Anyone who believes that an opposition would not do this has simply failed to grasp that one of the key roles of the opposition is to defeat the government.

The Chief, therefore, introduced an 'ordering motion' to change the sequence in which amendments would usually be debated. The amendments relating to abortion would come last, and ministers were instructed to give 'full and frank' answers to any queries that their colleagues raised when earlier amendments were being debated. MPs were, of course, encouraged to raise any issue of concern they might have. The technical name for this procedure is 'saving our colleagues from themselves', for, whatever the Chief or any other whip felt about the amendments, their prime job was to get the government's legislation through. The result was that the abortion amendments were never reached due to the shortage of time.

When things like this happen, you must remember one thing: you must never tell other people what is being planned. I was approached by many anxious (mainly Catholic) MPs who were desperate to know what was happening because they could not vote for the Bill if the amendments were passed. Of course, there were others who were desperate to vote for them, without realising that the whole Bill would likely be lost as a result. On such occasions, you must simply smile and tell people that 'it's all in hand'. To the very conscience-stricken who, in this case, included some who had voted against parts of the Bill earlier but, having lost, were prepared to give it a Third Reading, you are permitted to tell them they have no need to worry. If they have learnt to trust you, because you have spent sufficient time in the tea room talking to them, then they will believe you and stay quiet. What you must never do is to tell anyone how all this will be accomplished. Those who have tabled the propositions, if they have been around for some time, will realise that their amendments are unlikely to be reached and will shrug their shoulders, accepting defeat for the greater good. Those who do not realise what is going on will get very angry if you tell them and accuse the Whips' Office of being devious and reactionary. They are certainly right about the first part so there is no need to trouble them with information that they will find upsetting.

8. Princes and princesses

These are the people who are destined for greatness. They arrive from safe seats, often bequeathed to them at the last moment and which they have only just learnt how to find on a map. They are the chosen ones – destined, they believe, to become Prime Minister, probably in the near future. They certainly expect to be ministers after serving only the shortest possible time on the back benches.

You will not have to worry about their voting record because they will always vote with the government – after all, they want to be part of it. They will certainly not worry about any impact legislation may have on their constituencies since they seldom go there and, when they do, they have as little contact with normal people as possible. If they have previously lived outside London, which is usually the case only for Scottish MPs, they will de-camp to the capital as soon as possible. This is not so that they can be near Parliament, but so that they can be near the press. It is absolutely vital to them that they are always available to comment on a story, to review the papers or to be on television on a Sunday morning, when more sensible people are with their families, or at least having a lie-in, content to just *read* the papers.

Your problems with them will not be with their voting record, but with the fact that they see themselves as 'rising stars' – media shorthand for 'friends of mine who have got into Parliament'. Of course they are friendly with many political journalists – they have often worked with them or went to university with them; they frequently attend the same dinner parties. Journalists love them because they share the same preoccupations; rising property prices, London schools, the terrible cost of ballet lessons and extra language classes for their children. None of these things bother their constituents much, of course.

The trouble is that rising stars always have something more important to do than the routine business of the House of Commons. They will quickly find that sitting on statutory instrument committees, waiting for hours to speak in the Chamber, or being on the committee of a Bill that gets no publicity are all a waste of their valuable time. They always want to be away somewhere, addressing a conference, briefing the press about how dreadful life in the House of Commons is or attending an important dinner.

You, of course, are the lowest form of life. They are firm in the belief that, if you were any good, you would be in their shoes. If you have a regional accent, you are, by definition, a bit thick, suitable only for the grubbier, bullying side of politics. You know nothing about policy because you have never worked for a think tank or written any important articles in the Sunday press. So what can you tell them?

Firstly, you can make it clear in your unsubtle, bruising, whip's way, that people who wish to be promoted do as they are told and attend when they're asked. They will not believe you, of course, since they have far more important connections than you do, so find some way of retaliating. If they make a big drama about being asked to attend a committee (these are only for little people), then make sure that their next request for time off is refused. If they won't cooperate by speaking in a debate, find out what trip they want to go on. It's usually a visit to America, for these people love going to 'the States' or on visits to the UN. Then speak to the pairing whip and ask him to find a reason why they can't possibly go (the real reason being that you don't want them to go). It's even more effective if everyone else on the trip does get leave apart from this one individual.

They'll throw another wobbler, of course, but then you can retaliate by refusing another leave request. Make sure that the Chief and the Deputy are on your side and you can continue this war of attrition until even the dullest person gets the message. Although, so convinced are these people of their right to rule that it can often take some time. You can also add to their distress by putting them on committees you know they will hate and console yourself by remembering it will be the first time they have experienced what most people have to do at some point – putting up with a job they don't like. Consider it your contribution to their education.

Unfortunately, many of these people will become ministers eventually. They usually group together and have regular 'suppers' (London, not country). They promote one another and, together with admiring pieces written by journalists, their statements become a self-fulfilling prophecy. If everybody says X is very good, then it must be true and so X becomes a minister. They will always hold a grudge against you, but this needn't worry you too much. Firstly, you don't like them and they wouldn't like you anyway and, secondly, they'll all fall out eventually because not everyone can get the job they want. Watching these little groups form and fall apart is one of the mild amusements of parliamentary life. Of course, most of your colleagues loathe them too and so you'll gain brownie points by being difficult.

9. Friends

There is one more group of people you will have to learn to deal with as a whip: your friends. Remember as you do so that jobs come and go but you will always need friends, so try not to alienate them. At the same time, if you are going to be a good whip and if people in the parliamentary party are to trust you, you will have to be seen to be fair. So, giving them extra time off or covering up for them if they miss votes is not something you should do. However, all the advice about not going over the top in celebrating your new job or getting too self-important applies in spades to your dealings with your friends, and you should share your perks with them when you can. Usually this means offering them a lift home at night, or giving them a lift to or from the station in your government car. They will value this, especially at the end of a tough week or when they have heavy bags. You should also make the time to see your friends, to eat with them and to listen to all their frustrations. In doing this, you will have to accept that they will unload all their complaints about government policy and the way business is conducted onto you. This is not because they wish to spoil your evening, but because they will see you, probably entirely wrongly, as their conduit to the government and the top of the party. They mean well, so bear with them, especially if they are people who could have done a good job in government but have never been given the opportunity. If you have chosen your friends well, that will probably apply to most of them.

You are also permitted to tip them off if there are going to be no further votes on a particular day, or if you expect the business to end early. This allows them to have their meal early so that they can go home and get an early night now and then. They will not thank you if they are half-way through a meal in the dining room and are then told there will be no more votes.

For obvious reasons, it is important to be sure you get this information right. It will not look good for you if there are people explaining to the Deputy Chief Whip that they missed a vote because you had told them, wrongly, to go home. It's particularly important to get this right at the end of the week. Even if they don't actually leave earlier than anyone else, knowing that the business will finish early on a Thursday, and that they will be able to get a train home at a reasonable time, brightens people's week. If you tell them they will be able to get home early, and this doesn't happen, they will feel more miserable because they'll feel cheated. If you are sure of your ground though, let them know. They're your mates; give them that bit of pleasure.

Chapter 4

How to run the business

YOU'VE BEEN IN the House for a while, and you think that you know how the business works. When you are first appointed to the Whips' Office, you should disabuse yourself of this idea immediately. In the past, you may have looked at the Order Paper to see if you have a question, or to find out when a piece of business is starting because you are interested in participating. You will certainly have looked to see what time business is supposed to end and you can go home. Now you are a whip, you are starting all over again and you will need to read the Order Paper with a completely different eye because now you are looking out solely for trouble. Is there something at the end of the day where the opposition could call an unexpected vote? Is there an issue coming up which is likely to upset your own side? What about the timing? Does some business have to finish at a certain time if you want a vote on it or, more likely, must it go past a certain time to prevent a vote? All these things you will learn to recognise in time but, first, you will need to get a grip on the things that demand your immediate attention. The Deputy Chief Whip is paid to worry about the other problems so they need not concern you for a while.

Your first problem will be question time. The good news is that, on days when your department is not answering questions, you do not need to think about it at all. You are no longer allowed to ask a question, so you do not need to sit wracking your brains to find a way of raising a constituency issue or the vital topic of the day. However, to compensate for this inactivity, you will have a lot of work to do when the department you are responsible for is down to answer. First, you will need to make sure that enough of your own side are in the chamber to ask and answer questions, and that they have received briefings from ministers on suitable topics. Ministers are lonely and sensitive souls and do not like appearing in the House without a phalanx of supporters behind them. On some occasions, you may have to plead with people to leave the tea room and join you. Appealing to their better natures seldom works, especially if the minister is unpopular, so just ask them to do it as a favour to you.

You will also find that ministers or, to be accurate, their Special Advisors (Spads), are notoriously slow at producing briefings or produce very poor ones. Make sure that you have asked for the briefing several days before it is due and that you have checked it thoroughly. It is often the case that Spads produce suggested questions that are either insulting to other people's intelligence or could not possibly be asked on the floor of the House. The first is because they usually despise MPs, although generally aspiring to be one, and the second is because they never say the questions out loud and do not understand how ridiculous or long-winded they sound. Do not be afraid to demand changes. Spads think that they are cleverer than everyone else; they're not, which is why you are an MP and they aren't. In any case, you do not want to see decent people trying to ask a question they have been given and falling flat on their faces. They will only blame you.

Discourage eager Parliamentary Private Secretaries from scurrying around the chamber handing out briefings and never, ever do this yourself. All you will achieve is a shout of 'whip's plant' from the other side whenever one of your backbenchers stands up to ask a question. Briefings should always be given out discreetly and you should know who will need help to frame a suitable question and whether they are prepared to accept it. More importantly, you should know the people who can always be relied upon to ask a good question, whether they have used the briefing or not. Helpful and experienced backbenchers will either look at the briefing to find out what topics are current and then come up with their own question, or they will have a particular issue that they wish to raise. Others may need a bit of help simply because they are not experts in that area. Whatever you do, do not encourage the robotic reading-out of planted questions. It makes people look idiotic and brings politics into disrepute. People who cannot put two sentences together without a bit of paper in front of them should not have gone into politics in the first place.

Sensible ministers try to give full and proper answers to their own side and will recognise the interests and expertise of the person asking them the question. Listen to your ministers and, if they do not do this, you should ensure that you have a word with them afterwards. One day, they will need those backbenchers, and upsetting them is not a strategy for long-term survival. This is particularly true if someone has a local issue to raise. A good answer from the minister will find its way into the 'Anytown Gazette'; a bad one will ruin the local MP's planned press release and make him or her very cross with the minister. You should encourage people who want to raise a very local issue to tell you or the minister in advance, so that he or she is properly briefed. Once people realise that you are trying to make sure that they receive a decent answer, then they will be more than willing to cooperate, but you must make sure that they *do* get a decent answer. Ministers who do not answer properly or who, even worse, are rude to their own side, need to be pulled up sharply, reminded that the parliamentary party deserves better and that upsetting their own backbenchers is not a strategy for survival. If the minister won't listen to you, pass the problem on to the Deputy Chief Whip, who will make sure that someone more senior makes this clear. Sadly, there are some ministers who think that appearing in the House of Commons is a misuse of their time and that answering backbenchers diverts them from their more important tasks. Don't let them get away with this.

As well as managing question time, you will have to do your share of 'bench duty' every day. That is, you will take your turn sitting on the front bench, opposite the clerks and near to the Speaker, keeping an eye on what is going on. At busy times, ministers will try to persuade you to move, sometimes by the simple expedient of plonking themselves down on top of you. Stand your ground (or sit your ground). You are there to do a job and need to be where the Speaker and the clerks can talk to you and you to them. A good Deputy Chief Whip will have a very short way with ministers who try to move whips from their posts.

If you are the first person on duty during the day, you will need to collect the bench book from the whips' assistants and take it in with you. When you are taking over from another whip, he or she will hand it over. This lists the business and tells you what to say at any particular point when you need to speak. To ensure you don't miss anything vital, it will helpfully state in capital letters 'THE WHIP TO SAY', followed by what you have to read out. If you are new to the job, the Speaker or Deputy Speaker will usually give you a nod when you have to speak. None of it is difficult, and it is really idiot-proof, but you will still be terrified when you first have to do it, in case you somehow miss something and cause a major problem. A good way to deal with your fear and to lessen your terror is to regard yourself as an apprentice for the first few days of the job. Spend time sitting next to the whip who is on duty so that you can see how things really work in practice.

When you are on your own, the temptation during bench duty is to fall into a trance (hello birds, hello sky) because many of the debates you will have to sit through will be very, very boring. On occasions, you will find that you have planned your next holiday, drafted your shopping list or imagined how you would spend a lottery win, and been completely unaware of what has been going on around you for the last quarter of an hour. Try to resist this temptation, at least until you have been around long enough for your unconscious mind to rec-ognise warning signs and come back to earth. You might even have to listen to the speeches, but your consolation should be that, at least when you are bored, there is nothing going wrong. When it does, you will be glad if it is not on your watch.

Whether you are on bench duty or not, you should always make a habit of looking carefully through the Order Paper at the start of the day, keeping an eye out for potential problems. The Deputy Chief Whip will go through it each day before the start of business but, since you don't want to look a complete idiot, you will need to understand it and will soon learn to recognise the pressure points yourself.

If there is an urgent question, or a statement following question time, you will need to make sure plenty of your backbenchers turn up for it and you will be expected to be there yourself. Pull your weight in encouraging others to be there, even if your own department is not involved. There won't be much for you to do unless it is your own department making the statement or answering the question, in which case you treat it like question time and try to get your backbenchers to stand up. If you really can't be there, then make sure the Deputy Chief Whip knows why in advance. The one thing whips hate is a shirker, and you do not want to look like one. Moreover, you are expected to show solidarity with a minister who is dragged to the Commons to answer an unexpected question or to make a statement, especially if something has gone drastically wrong. Even if you believe the minister has been asking for trouble, as is sometimes the case, and you are fed up of dragging your colleagues in to defend the indefensible, recriminations have to be kept for inside the Whips' Office. Outside, you present a united front to the opposition.

On certain days, there will be a Ten Minute Rule Bill after questions. All MPs know that these are not real Bills and are not going anywhere, although some constituents get very exercised about them because they don't understand that. Usually, they are a way of allowing an MP either to raise a genuine issue or to ride their particular hobbyhorse. However, there are times when someone will decide to oppose the Bill and call a vote on it. There are generally only two reasons for this. The first is that an MP, or sometimes a group of MPs, objects violently to what is being proposed so they decide to call a vote to stop it going any further, even though they know it won't happen anyway. On these occasions, you must remember that the government does not have a view on what is being proposed, simply because it never has a view about a Ten Minute Rule Bill. MPs who decided to vote on it have a free vote, so resist the temptation to try to steer them into a particular lobby. This means that some poor souls will find themselves racked with indecision on these occasions and will be desperate to find out what the powers that be want them to do, in case voting the wrong way damages their promotion prospects. The truth is that the government doesn't care and neither should you. Let them make a decision for once. It's what MPs are supposed to do.

Your job is not to advise backbenchers how to vote, but you do have a role in keeping ministers out of the lobby. Despite the fact that they are frequently told not to vote on Ten Minute Rule Bills, there are some ministers who, like Pavlov's dogs, head for the lobby as soon as they hear the division bell, without any idea of what they are voting on. They cannot have a view, because the government doesn't have a view, so they should be gently, but firmly, turned around and kept out of the lobby. A few fail to grasp this essential fact of life, and will start to argue that they want to vote because they've had lots of emails from constituents. You can argue that, if they vote, they will put colleagues who have not voted in a very difficult position. Most will listen to that argument, as they accept collective responsibility, but there will always be a few selfish souls who carry on regardless. Sadly, there is nothing you can do except ensure that the Chief Whip knows that they have voted against your advice. He will then exact the appropriate revenge at the right time.

The other reason for calling a vote on this sort of Bill is simply to waste time, and it means that the Whips' Office, for some reason, does not want to reach a particular piece of business later in the day. It may be that there is an amendment to a Bill that would put the government in a difficult position, or one that would split the party, but, in either case, the aim is to use up as much time as possible on the preceding business. On one occasion, the Whips' Office was so determined not to reach a particular vote that the Chief Whip offered a bottle of champagne to the backbencher who could speak, and call a vote on, a Ten Minute Rule Bill. The offer was taken up and the champagne duly won, and drunk. This is another version of the procedure known as 'saving our colleagues from themselves', although it can become costly if used too often.

On days like that, the normal procedure is reversed. Far from trying to keep ministers out of the lobby, you will want them to vote. In fact, you want everybody to vote, although you are not really concerned which lobby they go into. This is very unsettling for a whip, but remember that all you are trying to do is use up as much time as possible. To that end, you should encourage people to linger in the lobby and have deep and meaningful conversations with their colleagues. You can feel free to buttonhole anyone you wish and keep them engaged for as long as possible. If all else fails, you can sit and talk to your fellow whips, but you will not leave until you have to. The aim is to drag it out for so long and you will know you have triumphed if the Speaker sends the serjeant-at-arms to 'investigate the delay in the lobby'. At that point you will have to give up and leave, but consider it a job well done and remember that the serjeant carries a sword.

The main business of the day will follow, either proceedings on a Bill, an opposition day or, sometimes, a debate 'on
the adjournment'. Adjournment Debates may be either trivial
or very serious. For example, they are often used to discuss
important foreign policy issues. On the other hand, so are
issues such as a general debate on Welsh Affairs. Issues like
this will not trouble you but on more important debates you
need to find out if someone will call a vote. This does not
often happen but there are occasions, for example a debate
on Iraq, where a group of people may decide to vote against
the adjournment at the end of the day as a way of expressing their concern or dissatisfaction with government policy.
Technically, they are voting against the House packing up and
going home at the end of the day but, if there are too many
from your own side, it can be embarrassing to the government and there will be a big effort to persuade people not to
vote and so reduce the number of 'rebels'.

On an opposition day, the topic for debate is chosen by
the other side and the government will want to ensure that
there are enough people in the chamber speaking against the
opposition motion and that they are all there to vote at the end.
Most of the work will be done by the whip whose department
is answering the debate. You need not worry too much about
this unless it is your department, in which case you should
worry a great deal and you will have to beg or persuade enough
people to speak.

If government legislation is being debated, you will learn
of the terrors of the parliamentary timetable and why debates

sometimes have to be spun out so that the votes do not come early.

If it is the Second Reading of a Bill, you will know exactly when the vote is going to be and things are relatively straight-forward. However, if it is your department's legislation, more will be expected from you.[2] It is usually important that the debate doesn't finish early so, if there aren't enough speak-ers, all whips will be asked to help find some.

As a backbencher, you will have experienced intense annoy-ance when this happens, wondering why the debate had to be spun out so that votes did not come early to allow you to go home. Now you are a whip, you will understand the reason. When a vote is due at a particular time, many of your colleagues will not arrive until just before the division bells ring. Indeed, some of them cut it so fine that they are hurling themselves into the lobby just before the door closes. Some may have only just arrived from their constituencies, especially at the begin-ning of the week. Others will have been around earlier in the day and then gone out.

The risk in having an early vote is that the opposition may bring all their people back to ambush you, knowing that not all your people will be there. This is not likely to happen often, especially when the government has a big majority, but, when it does, the consequences are disastrous and therefore the first rule of a whip's life is to 'take no risks'. If it looks like the debate might finish early, all whips will be sent out to

---

find people to speak and keep it going, encouraging your side to make long speeches, rounding up from the tea room those people who are always eager to share their thoughts with the world and let them have free rein. Old hands and those who know the score will hide away, unwilling to waste one of their precious speaking opportunities on a subject in which they have no interest, only to find that they are not called when they wish to be. Forget about them and trawl the library and the cafeterias, seeking out the long-winded and those keen to make an impression. Those who feel the nation is ever-eager for their views on any subject can be drafted in. If there are not enough of them, dig out those who owe you a favour, or beg your friends. Some people are specialists in this kind of thing. Stephen Pound, for instance, can speak on almost any subject with little warning and be warm and entertaining. Unfortunately, not many people have his talent, so you will end up 'owing' a number of people for getting you out of a hole when they would appreciate an early night. Since the Chief Whip will not appreciate having to explain to the Prime Minister why a piece of government legislation has failed to get through Parliament, you will just have to pay your debts.

Only when there is a completely uncontentious piece of business being debated, and only when the opposition spokesperson has said publicly from the front bench that they will not be opposing it, should you be relaxed about a debate finishing early. Even then, make sure that someone from your own side is not going to call a vote.

At the end of the day's business, there will be various other motions on the agenda, and you need to make sure that there are none that can be voted on. There are always several of these and they may look harmless, but some are debateable and, if the main business finishes early, some may be voteable when that happens. In particular, some things are debateable before 10 p.m., or 7 p.m. (or whatever time the main business would normally finish), but not afterwards. Scrutinise them carefully and watch out for the traps. Some will be things that the government wants to sneak through quietly. Others will be on issues that obsess a small number of people who would like to debate them until the small hours. Remember that there are many eagle-eyed MPs who have been at the game much longer than you and who will spot these things. However much you might sympathise with their desire to have a debate or a vote, you now represent the forces of darkness and so your job is to stop them. These eager debaters are yet another reason why finishing business early is a bad idea.

Chapter 5

Looking after a Bill

JUST WHEN YOU think that you have got to grips with managing the daily business, the department to which you have so lovingly attached yourself is bound to produce a Bill. It will be your job to steer it through the House intact. If you are lucky, it will be a well-drafted, popular piece of legislation – at least with your own colleagues. However, you will seldom get that lucky. Drafting errors in government Bills are legendary, leading to the need for lots of government amendments later down the line, and departments have the unfortunate habit of either producing Bills that MPs don't like much, or trying to slip in things that civil servants have wanted to legislate on for ages in the hope that no one notices.

It is your job to notice, so, when legislation is on its way, make sure that you are invited to all the departmental meetings that discuss it and that ministers keep you fully briefed. They are often not keen on this, as they see the Bill as their baby, which they will nurture gently into adulthood. You should point out that it will be still-born unless they get MPs on side and that it is your job to help them do this. Some ministers have a remarkable ability to adopt the department's priorities as their own and think that getting parliamentary support is just a minor inconvenience that the Whips' Office can easily sort out. Remember that you are not there to comment on the contents of the Bill or to try to get changes to it (much as you might like to), but to spot the elephant traps that are going to cause trouble for your own side. Point out immediately if there is something that will be difficult to get through the House and make sure that you alert the Chief Whip to any potential problems. He can try to head off some of the worst disasters, but only inside the Whips' Office will you ever be able to give vent to your feelings and say that you think a proposal is stupid.

Good ministers prepare the ground for legislation by talking to MPs with expertise in the subject and discussing potential difficulties. Bad ministers think that they can come up with anything and it is the duty of the whips to get it through. Ministers who wish to be especially devious will try to hide some of their intentions from you, and may even introduce controversial amendments at a late stage. You can try to avoid being ambushed like this by getting to know the Bill team and attending some of their meetings. These are the civil servants delegated to work on the Bill, and they are very useful sources of information. You should be sure that you are on good terms with the person in charge so that you can ring them up for a chat at any time. They will let you know how the drafting is progressing but, because they are not politicians, they will often fail to see the problems it might face in Parliament. The upside is that, because they are unaware of these problems, they will seldom try to hide things from you. They will also know the legislation very well and will be happy to explain anything you do not understand. You should not be afraid of asking them, especially if you are now working in an area where you have no real expertise. Someone else in Parliament certainly will and ignorance will not lead to bliss.

Once the Bill is published, you will need to get to know it thoroughly. Take it home with you and read it, along with the explanatory notes. When the library produces its briefing on the Bill, which is usually a little while after publication, read that as well. You are looking for the pressure points, things that might upset your own side or that could cause you problems in Committee Stage. You should also listen very carefully to what your colleagues say about it so that you are aware of the reaction on your own back benches. If you detect problems, make sure that you mention them in the whips' meeting so that others can keep their ears open too. Some of your difficulties can be solved by a simple explanation of why a certain course of action is needed, so make sure that the minister in charge of the Bill speaks to anyone who has concerns. Other problems may be genuine ones that no one in the department has yet spotted, in which case they can often be dealt with by a government amendment, or one moved by a backbencher and which the government can accept, either during the Committee Stage or at the Report Stage of the Bill. If someone is an expert on the particular issue involved and has spotted a problem, it's nice to let them move the amendment so that they get some credit for the work. If a minister insists on a government amendment, try to make sure that he or she gives due acknowledgement to the people that raised the issue in the first place. They will feel better because of it. Above all, make sure that your minister listens to and engages with all of the people who have genuine expertise in the area. They can help, and they are useful allies if they know they are being taken seriously.

At Second Reading, you will need to tell the Deputy Chief Whip how many speakers there are on both sides. He will also prefer it if your side has more speakers than your opponents, or at least will want to know that they are equal. Get yourself along to the Speaker's office prior to the meeting and they will give you a list of the speakers on your side and tell you how many opposition speakers there are. If there are not enough people on your side who have put in to speak, then you should go into action immediately, along with the minister's Parliamentary Private Secretary (PPS). Contact your friends, call in favours, promise them almost anything, beg if you have to, but do not go into your daily meeting without having enough speakers for the debate to continue through its allotted time. You will look incompetent and other whips will be asked to assist in finding speakers. This is one of those occasions when you need your friends. Ask them to save you from this humiliation.

You will get a good idea of how your own side are responding to the Bill. You are not concerned about the opposition and their objections, although the civil servants on the Bill team often are and will relay some of their comments to you. Tell them you are not bothered and concentrate on your own side. You are in government because your party can out-vote all the others as long as your own side stick with you. Your job is to make sure that they do. Civil servants will be shocked by this attitude, but remember that you are a whip and they are civil servants precisely because you see the world differently.

You will then have to find people to serve on the Bill committee. There will be some who want to do it because they are genuinely interested in the subject and want to engage constructively in the process. You should encourage them, because you will not have trouble getting them to turn up. Others will want to be there to make trouble and will certainly attend regularly but only to cause mayhem, so avoid them at all costs.

Unless your legislation is very popular, the rest of your committee will be made up of people who have to be persuaded, bribed or dragooned into agreeing to serve. This, of course, is where the careerists come in useful. How many fall into each category and how much persuading you have to do will depend on the nature of the Bill. Some legislation is popular and interesting, and you will have no trouble filling your committee. If it is popular but boring, you can usually persuade people to let their names go forward on the understanding that there will be no late nights and that they can sit at the back and answer their post or write speeches. You need not feel bound by these promises once you have got them there – you're a whip. In fact, few politicians, faced with the spectacle of their opponents in full flow, can resist the temptation to get up and speak. You are really doing them a favour and allowing them to give their thoughts on a matter of national importance, even if the country is not listening.

When a piece of legislation is really unpopular, either with a section of the public or with MPs, or if the committee is taking place at an awkward time, then you will have to rely on those trying to climb the greasy pole and those who owe you a favour. Contrary to popular opinion, politicians do recognise obligations, so reminding people of when you helped them out by speaking in a debate for them, meeting their constituents or visiting their constituency, usually works wonders. Others will recognise their obligations to the party. When I had to steer the Bribery Bill through committee just before the general election, most people wanted to be away in their constituencies so the Bill was carried through by MPs who were retiring as their contribution to helping the government and their colleagues. One or two may have owed me a favour as well!

Once the committee begins, you should remember that you will need a majority there at all times. You may think that nothing much is going to happen, but if the opposition whip spots that you no longer have a majority, you can be certain he or she will take advantage of it. Often, your colleagues (especially ministers) will want to miss sessions of the committee on the grounds that they have something more important to do. Ministers are especially prone to this when there is more than one minister working on the Bill, and seldom see why two of them should be there at the same time. Tell them that you need their votes and do not listen to pleas that 'my section doesn't come up until later in the week'. Make it clear that they may work just outside the door of the committee room, but they must be there to vote when you need them. For this reason, they must not wander off down the corridor, go to meet anyone in central lobby or otherwise stray away from the sound of your voice. It is surprising how many ministers fail to understand these simple instructions, or believe that they do not apply to them. Remind them that it is their legislation you are trying to get through and that, if they are unwilling to turn up and vote for it, there is no reason why backbenchers should.

Other members of your committee will need a break from time to time, to go to the loo or to get a coffee or just to prevent the cabin fever that can come from being in a committee room for hours on end. Try to establish early on that there should only be one person outside at a time and that they should get the nod from you before they leave. If a vote is due, ask them to hang on for a while. Most people are very cooperative about this as long as they know you are trying to be fair to everyone. For the same reason, be wary about giving time off to the first person who asks you. You can try to accommodate reasonable requests for absence, when someone has a very important event to attend, especially from those who are there as a favour to you, but you must never lose your majority. Others may have a good reason to want to be away on a particular day, so you should grant absences only if there is no alternative, attendance at a funeral, for example, or a minister visiting the constituency.

You will find that the whole process will be simpler if you explain to everyone how you intend to run the committee right from the start. This allows people to plan what they are doing and makes life easier for everyone. The opposition will attempt to delay things and you need to have the Bill out of committee by a set date. These two aims are irreconcilable so make sure that you are the one in control. You do not want large parts of it not debated, as this will increase the chances of people getting their amendments selected at Report Stage, thus causing you trouble on the floor of the House, so you need to make progress. If the opposition delay things too much, dragging out debates and making long speeches, tell them you intend to keep the committee sitting late until you have reached a particular clause in the Bill. Since only the government whip can move the adjournment of the committee, this puts you in a powerful position, but you can only do this if you have worked out in advance how much you need to get through each day. If you tell your committee members in advance when you might have to sit late, it helps them and ensures that they are not cheesed off with you because they had plans for that evening. Make sure that they know they should not reveal your plan to the opposition. Some people can be astonishingly naive.

Unless your Bill is really in dire straits, you will not want to keep the committee sitting late on a Thursday night. You will prevent people from getting home at a decent hour and possibly ruin their plans for a constituency Friday. They will have to cancel constituency engagements, which always makes an MP very unpopular since constituents never understand that MPs are elected to be in the House of Commons rather than turn up at village fetes or to open things. Your colleagues will then blame you for their unpopularity, and they will be right, since you should never let a Bill get so behind schedule in the first place. On Tuesdays, you can use the threat of sitting late on a Thursday to force the opposition to make some progress and you can keep them late if necessary, but they will only believe your threats if you have convinced them from the start that you are a mean bastard who will give no quarter, which, in this case, ought to be true.

One committee that was lumbered with a garrulous (and not very bright) opposition frontbencher started to get through the various clauses much more quickly after I had informed the Tory whip that I would not adjourn it until we reached a certain clause, however long that might take. The shadow minister in question, who had been droning on interminably about very minor points up until then, suddenly rediscovered the virtues of short and pithy speeches. Your own side will support you in this, even if it means being there later on a Tuesday, since they find this infinitely preferable to being late on a Thursday – not to mention that they will be fed up with the opposition droning on as well. The opposition whip will, no doubt, tell you that there is plenty of time and that things will speed up after they have made some very important points on a particular clause. Do not believe him. His job is to delay the Bill, and yours is to get it through the committee in the time allowed. These two aims are fundamentally incompatible, and it is a fight that you must win. If parts of the Bill are not debated in committee then the opposition can, justifiably, ask for more time at the Report Stage to debate them. This mucks up the government's legislative timetable and you do not want to be the person who has to explain this to the Chief Whip. So have no truck with these suggestions from your opposite number. Keep to the timetable, which you should have in your head, and things will proceed more smoothly.

Your own minister may not want to sit late since, as I've said, some ministers believe that they have far more important things to do than getting the government's legislation through. If so, you should remind them that this is their job and attending an important dinner somewhere is not their main task. The opposition will hate it because one of the reasons they try to drag things out is that the shadow minister is not prepared for the next stage of the Bill. This is entirely understandable, since opposition is a hard job and shadow ministers are often working on their own, while the government ministers have a host of civil servants and some Spads to explain the provisions of the Bill and help them prepare their speeches. You may sympathise, but this is hard luck and you should give no quarter and insist on pressing on. One day, the same thing is likely to happen to you as the wheel of politics turns and life, especially political life, is never fair.

When your Bill finishes Committee Stage, there is usually a pause before it returns to the floor of the House for its Report Stage and Third Reading. This may lull you into a false sense of security and you may believe that you have no work to do. You are wrong. People will start to table amendments for the Report Stage almost immediately, and so you should get copies of these every day from the Vote Office and make sure that you understand them. If any come from your own side, talk to the proposer and find out if there is a serious issue that the minister needs to address, and remember that there will be some people who are experts in whatever field you are dealing with, or who have campaigned on an issue for a long time. It is your job to make sure that they are taken seriously and that any problems they raise are dealt with properly. On the Welfare Reform Bill, for example, one of my colleagues had been campaigning vigorously for blind people to have access to the higher rate mobility component of DLA. He had raised this in committee, but did not press his amendment to the vote because ministers had promised to look at the issue. He tabled it again at Report Stage and made it clear that he would press it to a vote if ministers did not take action.

Junior ministers were sympathetic, but it was clear that action was being blocked somewhere along the line. After getting nowhere by encouraging negotiations, I had to tell the Secretary of State bluntly that there was absolutely no chance that we could whip Labour MPs through the lobby to deny giving blind people access to this benefit. He had a choice between accepting the amendment or being defeated on the floor of the House. Since the Secretary of State at the time was the totally detached James Purnell, I am ashamed to say that I took great pleasure in doing so. He gave in and the law was changed. It was a fine example of a good campaign waged by someone who cared deeply about the issue and who had right on his side. You should always treat people like this with respect and make sure you do what you can to help them. You can justify your partisanship by remembering that you are saving the government from defeat and preventing ministers damaging their own reputations. No one wants 'I denied benefits to blind people' as their political epitaph, and that includes you. Just make sure that you have the backing of the Chief Whip before you threaten a minister with defeat.

It is very important that you find out which of your own members will want to press an amendment to the vote and which are simply looking to raise an issue and get some reassurance from the minister. Most fall in to the latter category and you should do your best to see that ministers are aware of their concerns and are ready to deal with them. A good minister will continue to engage with people who have serious issues to raise, even at this late stage of the Bill, while bad ones tend to dismiss even their own colleagues. It's your job to make sure that doesn't happen, and that ministers meet people like this and are prepared to give them proper answers during the debate. What you should also be aware of is that the government will also table amendments. Many of these will be simply to correct drafting errors, but some will address points raised in committee, or implement an assurance when a minister has undertaken to deal with a particular issue at Report Stage. The ones that should ring alarm bells are rarer, but much more troublesome, when ministers try to put into the Bill a proposal that they know will be contentious and unpopular with their own side, but have been holding back until now in the hope that it will be too late for real opposition to get going. They are almost always wrong about this and trouble will certainly be on its way. You should let the Chief Whip know immediately if you get wind of anything like this, just in case he doesn't know already, as dealing with it is well above your pay grade. If the government has decided to go ahead with something unpopular, you will have to try to deliver the votes, but if the minister is trying to sneak something in on his own initiative, then it can often be stopped. The perpetually difficult James Purnell, for example, tried to put into the Welfare Reform Bill the final sanction of complete loss of benefit while it was going through the Lords. The amended Bill would have had to come back to the Commons for approval and chaos would result. It was widely suspected that he was doing so to cause trouble for Gordon Brown. It was stopped.

On the day that your Bill is back on the floor, you will need to get the Speaker's final selection of amendments as soon as they appear, which is usually around lunchtime, and mark them up for your colleagues. You can usually get a draft from the clerks but the final selection will only appear an hour or two before the debate starts. You will then need to produce a colour-coded copy, using different colours for government amendments, opposition amendments and amendments from your own backbenchers. This has to be distributed to your fellow whips at the daily meeting before the start of business and you will be expected to take them through the list, pointing out any items that may cause particular problems and telling them where you expect votes. You will need to talk to the opposition whip in advance to ask him what they intend to call a vote on. Sometimes he will tell you, since whips on all sides like the business to run smoothly. If he says he doesn't know, then prepare for a vote. The rule in dealing with whips on the opposite side is that you must never lie to one another, but you don't have to reveal everything. It is better to be prepared for a vote that does not come than to be unprepared for one that does, so you should always be cautious.

You will also need to know from your own ministers whether there are any amendments that they are prepared to accept. Some are notoriously bad at making decisions on things like that, and one serial offender was even known to say that he would 'listen to the debate'. This is a parliamentary term that means 'I haven't got a clue' and you must refuse to put up with it. Whips can't work like that and you should insist on a decision. Tell ministers that if they cannot make up their minds, you cannot guarantee having sufficient people there to support them when they finally do. Bring in pressure from the Chief Whip or the Deputy Chief Whip if they insist on being difficult.

Once proceedings begin, you should never go far from the chamber and should try to be on the bench for most of the time. The whips on bench duty will not know the Bill as well as you do and will not understand the various amendments. You should also make sure that you know the order in which the votes will come, as this is not the same as the order in which amendments are debated, and you should keep an eye on timing so that votes that the government wishes to reach actually take place (or vice-versa). A good minister will appreciate that you are doing your job, and you can hope that it is not necessary to go as far as one whip who passed a note to a particularly long-winded minister that read: 'Shut the fuck up now.'

It is absolutely vital that you are there at the time of a vote so that the whip on bench duty knows whether to shout 'aye' or 'no'. Other people on your side will follow that lead, and those in a hurry will head for the appropriate lobby immediately, so you do not want to be responsible for the chaos that follows if it all goes wrong. Be around to help steer people into the right lobby and to answer any questions. After all, you have steered the Bill this far and you should now understand it as well as anyone.

Third Reading will come after Report Stage and is usually led by the Secretary of State, who turns up at this point like the woman who used to arrive at the end of a *Morecambe and Wise* show. It may sound obvious, but make sure that he or she is there in good time. Some ministers make a career of cutting it fine. Indeed, one, very well thought of by the party, once missed the Third Reading of his own Bill because he was chatting to someone in the corridor! He was in the building, had been around for the Report Stage, but had wandered off after a vote. Instead of his carefully prepared speech, the Third Reading was moved formally by the whip on bench duty and was over in a flash. The whip was not happy, nor were the senior whips, and the departmental whip had learnt an important lesson – once you have your minister there, keep an eye on them and do not let them wander off. Such behaviour is unforgivable and, despite this particular minister's glowing reputation, he was considered to be a complete prat by the Whips' Office from then on.

If there is a vote at the end of Third Reading, you need to remind your ministers that two of them should be standing by the voting desks in the division lobby to thank colleagues for supporting their legislation. (If there isn't a vote, they should do this at the last vote on Report Stage.) This is an old-fashioned courtesy that some people tend to forget about, but it is seen by MPs as an acknowledgement of the part they have played. You should be there too. No Bill would go through without the support of the back benches and no whip can do their job without cooperation from them. Show your gratitude and they will be more willing to help you in the future.

You will then go home with a sigh of relief as you see the Bill off to the Lords and hope that it returns unamended, glad to have seen the last of that particular piece of legislation and looking forward to getting a little more time to yourself. Enjoy it while you can. That hope will be frequently dashed as, after the Bill has gone through the Lords, it is likely to return with amendments for you to deal with. Still, for that night, your work is done.

Chapter 6

Ministers and ex-ministers

YOU ARE A minister in Her Majesty's Government, but no one will ever treat you as one. First of all, remember that some of the ministers you deal with will actively despise whips. Those who have served in the Whips' Office themselves are usually, but not always, an exception to this rule (some of them even acquire VIMS – Very Important Minister Syndrome), as are the sensible souls who understand how Parliament actually works. However, you may as well accept from the start that a number of them will hold the firm view that whips are a lower form of life and that, if you were any good, you would be in a department, slogging away at the end of some long corridor as Parliamentary

Under-Secretary for Paperclips. The idea that some people enjoy the Whips' Office and might even *want* to be there has never entered their heads. It's because they really don't like Parliament much. Many of these people got elected not to be MPs, but to be ministers, which is why they often drift away when opposition looms. They love their daily round of visits and meetings, they are seldom in the House, except when trouble is looming, and then they wonder who all the people around them are. The sight of a group of ministers who hardly ever talk to their colleagues suddenly arriving in an attempt to head off a rebellion, desperate to buy their colleagues a coffee and to talk to them, brings a smile to the face of even the most hardened MP. Don't worry about them, because you will soon learn to despise them as much as they despise you.

When you arrive in the Whips' Office, as well as being given your 'flock' of backbench MPs to look after, you will be assigned your own department. You will then be responsible for seeing all of that department's legislation through Parliament and ensuring that its ministers are there to vote when they are needed. There will be some ministers who appreciate that you are there to help them, who will make sure that you are included in all their departmental meetings and that you are aware of any legislation which they are planning to bring forward well in advance. If you are assigned to a department run by a Secretary of State who takes this attitude, then be thankful. These are a rare species and you should be grateful for them. Remember that your job is not to comment on the contents of the legislation, much as you will be tempted to do so. Your task is to talk to the other ministers about how to get it through Parliament, pointing out the difficulties they may encounter and how these can be dealt with. These sensible ministers will listen to you, give due weight to what you say, and act on your recommendations, recognising that you are simply trying to avoid trouble.

If you are unfortunate enough to be attached to a department where ministers don't understand this, then you will face problems. There are those in every government who believe that it is the role of the whips to force through any legislation they come up with, however ludicrous or unpopular it may be. These ministers believe that you have a magic wand that can make rebellions disappear. They should be immediately disabused of that idea. If their own side have doubts about what they are bringing forward, it is their job to talk to MPs about it and try to convince them. Tell them that the 'black book' doesn't exist and so bribery is out, and remind them that if they can't persuade their own side to support them then their legislation might, just possibly, be flawed. They may also be inclined to believe that your own backbenchers are the enemy, so it is occasionally necessary to gently point out that these are their colleagues, even if they do not take a red box home every night.

Ministers who resent having a whip attached to their department usually regard you as a spy for the Chief Whip or the Prime Minister, and they are right on both counts – that's your job. They will change the times of departmental meetings without telling you so that you will walk up to the department (often when you are very busy) to find the meeting has been cancelled. At other times, it will be held without you being informed. They will be very apologetic when you raise this and blame their private office. Do not fall for this. A private office acts on the instruction of a minister, and either the civil servants have not been instructed to tell you or they have been clearly instructed not to. Either of these things should worry you. Another tactic is to hold meetings but ensure that nothing of importance is discussed while you are there. Alarm bells should ring then, because it means that the important topics are being debated elsewhere. You should give the Secretary of State a chance to put this right by making it plain that you will not be able to help unless he takes you into his confidence, that you are aware of what is happening and that losing a government Bill will not be good for his career. A minister who is acting out of sheer ignorance will listen to this. Unfortunately, ignorance is not likely to be the reason for excluding you.

Shocking though it may be to hear, some ministers actually plot against the Prime Minister who appointed them. That is why, shortly after I became a whip, I was told that I was going to the Department for Work and Pensions, where James Purnell was the Secretary of State. James was a media darling, thought of by the London press as one of the 'intellectuals' of the government, an image which he assiduously cultivated. He had come into Parliament on what MPs scathingly referred to as 'the assisted places scheme'. Having worked for Tony Blair, he was sent on secondment to work for Tom Pendry, who was due to retire as the MP for Stalybridge and Hyde. Of course, it worked. Labour Party members are surprisingly trusting. James was undoubtedly bright – destined to be a minister – and had the irritating habit of always looking over your shoulder when he spoke to you, in case someone more important came along. Many Labour MPs loathed him and instinctively distrusted any legislation he might bring forward. My job was to keep an eye on him and to try to head off trouble. I had to ensure that the Welfare Reform Bill went through, despite the fact that he was in charge of it and, in the Chief's words, 'find out what he's up to and stop it'. The first was manageable; the second would require constant vigilance. Bearing all this in mind, outside the Whips' Office being given such a job would look like a punishment. It wasn't. It was seen as a compliment, a sign that I was trusted to do a good job and prevent trouble. Always remember this if you are asked to do something difficult and remember that easy jobs are given to people regarded as incompetent. They may have an easy life, but they will not last long.

James was a master of all the evasive tactics I have described above and I had to go and see the Chief Whip to tell him that departmental meetings were regularly being cancelled. A good Chief will not see this as a failure on your part, but will realise that something is going on that he needs to know about. You must tell the Chief if you suspect any minister of disloyalty, even if it is someone you like. Remember, that is the duty you have to the Prime Minister who appoints you.

Spotting people who are disloyal is relatively easy. It is far harder to spot ministers who are working on legislation that they believe in absolutely, but which is likely to destabilise the party and lead to a government defeat. As in the old joke about the Home Office, not only do you not know who they are, but they do not know who they are. Nevertheless, you must find them.

Ministers are frequently told by their civil servants that a particular action or piece of legislation is essential for the greater good. Sometimes, these Bills have been lurking in the department for years until a minister comes along who is gullible enough to take one up without asking why none of his predecessors did so. New ministers are particularly susceptible to the 'greater good' argument, as they are eager to make a good start with their civil servants and are often told that the previous minister was 'just about to approve it' when the reshuffle took place. You might wonder how such trusting individuals become ministers, but sometimes they do. Bear in mind also that some do not want to offend their civil servants, who report back on them through the network of permanent secretaries to the Cabinet Secretary, who may then insinuate to the Prime Minister that they are 'not up to the job' or 'lazy'. Until Prime Ministers are prepared to treat these reports with a large dose of scepticism, there will always be ministers who do not want to take on the Whitehall machine. Unfortunately, the machine takes no account of the need to get legislation through Parliament. That is your job.

So, when you sit in departmental meetings, be on the alert for things that may cause trouble in the future. They may only be mentioned casually and spoken about as if everyone understands what is happening. You will not, so don't be afraid to ask for more information. You will, no doubt, be treated with the disdain that the civil service believes that you deserve, but it is far better to be thought a fool than to prove you are one. Usually, these little time bombs are being handled in some innocuous-sounding committee within the department, with little thought for the parliamentary process that most civil servants seem to consider an unnecessary waste of time. Good ministers will find out what's going on and head off trouble early. When they don't, you are the last line of defence.

You should remember that ministers and civil servants love legislation. It raises the profile of the department and makes them look active and important. No minister ever made a reputation by looking around and saying, 'You know, this seems to be working OK. Let's just keep an eye on it.' They want to show how active and forward-thinking they are, and so departments fight for slots in the legislative timetable and feel downgraded if they haven't got enough legislation. What is more, ministers sometimes make promises without any idea of how they can be fulfilled. Since it is your job to make these promises a reality by getting the legislation through Parliament, you will naturally hope that they think before making them. Dream on.

The Ministry of Justice, to which I was sent after my stint at the Department for Work and Pensions, seemed especially prone to these grand gestures and, because it was responsible for a number of organisations that MPs hate, especially prone to get them riled. For example, at one weekly whips' meeting, we were informed that Jack Straw had promised a pay rise of 40 per cent to both the Information Commissioner and the head of the Electoral Commission. When this was announced, the assembled whips all simultaneously raised their eyes to heaven and invoked the deity. The reason was simple. The Information Commissioner had already ruled that certain details of expenses had to be published, which did not make him the most popular person in Parliament, and MPs hated the Electoral Commission with a passion. They considered its members to be a useless bunch with no knowledge whatsoever of how elections are run. Since, at the time, the only qualification for being a member was that a person had never stood for elected office, I thought that was a fair summary. In fact, I considered it fairly mild, given that I had needed to have an Adjournment Debate to force them to take notice of significant failures by the Returning Officer in Warrington, and that they usually failed to answer my letters, which was a serious offence, probably deserving of capital punishment or, at least, complete abolition.

Now we were expected to get MPs to vote to give these people a pay rise. The real issue, though, was the size of the pay rise. And we had to do it in the middle of an economic crisis, when people were losing their jobs. 'Forty per cent,' muttered one whip. 'For fuck's sake.' (Language deteriorates once you become a whip.) The fact that we were being asked to do this when MPs had seen their own pay held down, because the government would never implement the recommendations of the independent review body that was supposed to set their pay, made it worse. What was more, all ministers, including the whips, had been instructed not to accept any pay rise awarded to them, including any rise in their parliamentary salary. This meant we were actually taking a pay cut, since pension contributions were deducted as if we were getting the higher salary. This might not have meant much to people on a Cabinet minister's salary, but it did to those in the lower ranks. We knew we were much better off than many people, but not getting the rise you were actually awarded would rankle with most people and we were no different. Despite what many think, we are human.

Even worse, everyone knew that the economic crisis meant that there would be no rise in the foreseeable future, yet quangocrats they loathed were to get a huge increase. MPs see an unelected group of people, often exercising powers they believe should belong to Parliament, appointing one another to lucrative jobs and moving from one post to another, even if they mess up. The feeling that a self-perpetuating oligarchy of well-off Londoners were taking decisions that affected many people's lives had grown stronger with time, and yet ministers seemed totally unaware of it. After all, they met these people regularly, they had lunch with them. What could possibly be wrong?

The Chief Whip stopped the string of complaints with a question: 'Does anyone believe that we can get this through?' He went around the table. One by one, the whips shook their heads. 'No.'

We did, of course, because we had to. That was our job. After much to-ing and fro-ing and many postponements, we had to accept that we couldn't get rid of it. Jack Straw insisted that he had given personal assurances to those involved and that a senior minister could not be seen to go back on his word. Junior ministers, of course, do this all the time, usually when they are taking the flak for someone more senior. By the time the proposal came to Parliament, MPs were fighting on too many fronts, so we put it through late at night after most people had gone home and I'd now like to make a formal apology to my colleagues for this action. It left a nasty taste, with MPs feeling undervalued and driven into a corner. That's not the way you want them to be feeling in times of trouble, and trouble was certainly coming.

To cheer the troops up even further, the department put forward the Political Parties and Elections Bill, a piece of legislation that had too many things wrong with it to list and which was so badly drafted that it caused normally stalwart supporters of the government to vote against the whip. One of the original proposals would have allowed the Electoral Commission to enter and search MPs' homes and offices. No doubt this had seemed a great idea to a civil servant some-where. They could cut out the middle-man, save all the bother of going to the police, producing evidence and having the police apply to a magistrate for a search warrant. Not surpris-ingly, the idea that we should give this spectacularly useless organisation powers the country did not even allow its police force went down badly with MPs. Jaws dropped all around the table when the assembled whips found out, realising that backbenchers would (rightly) be incandescent with rage.

Eventually we got rid of the idea through continuous lobbying and convincing the Prime Minister that it would never get through the House. Yet, the fact that these proposals had come from a department where the Secretary of State was generally thought to be a safe pair of hands, who actually *liked* the House of Commons, spent time there and was willing to engage with his colleagues, showed how easy it was for a minister to become detached from what was going on outside his particular bubble.

Of course, our thoughts about this were kept strictly inside the office, the only safe space where you are allowed to let off steam. Occasionally, Tony Cunningham (our pairing whip) would plaintively call, 'Why is it always Jack?' from his desk at the end of the room.

This would be the cue for a chorus, like a parliamentary version of a Greek tragedy.

'Freedom of Information?'

'Jack...'

'P.R. for Euro elections?'

'Jack.'

'Political Parties Bill?'

'Jack!'

We could have gone on.

Indeed, we were so fed up that, when I proposed the idea of a new Bill to be called the 'Jack Straw (Repeal) Bill', it was adopted unanimously. The Bill would only have one clause, we decided: 'Any legislation introduced by the Rt Hon. Member for Blackburn in any capacity whatsoever is hereby repealed.'

Granted, that would mean a lot of criminal justice Bills might fall, but, since we seemed to have a new one every other week, we weren't too bothered.

These lamentations, of course, never left the Whips' Office. Outside, the whips always support government legislation, however barmy it might be.

Apart from introducing troublesome legislation, one of the worst sins a minister can commit in the eyes of the whips is to be 'lazy'. Of course, most ministers are not lazy in the normal sense of the word. They work long hours and often deal with their red boxes late into the night. They are never off-duty and in some departments, like Defence, are woken in the middle of the night more often than anyone realises. They work at weekends too. Yet, whips have little sympathy for them. After all, they too work long hours, are constantly on call, and also get late-night phone calls. 'Lazy' to a whip means something different. It denotes a minister who does not pull his or her weight in the House.

Some ministers will tell you that they need to be let off a vote because they are 'tired' or have an early start in the morning. This is the parliamentary equivalent of saying that your hamster has died, and you should take no notice of it. You will be tired, the backbenchers will be tired, so remind them that they are paid more because they are expected to do more, and refuse to plead their case with the pairing whip. You might, if someone is being particularly difficult, remind them that backbenchers have to stick around to put through their legislation and cannot be expected to do so if ministers slope off early. Now that the House has changed its hours, late-night votes occur less frequently, but this government doesn't have much legislation to put through. Another government probably will have and those who expected seven o'clock votes to continue to be the end of their day for most of the week are likely to be disappointed.

You can bet, however, that whatever the time of the vote, some ministers will try to get away. One minister told the pairing whip, during a long night, that he was going home. 'You can't,' was the reply. The minister insisted. He had cleared it with his Secretary of State; he had a lot of important work to do. 'No,' said the pairing whip, pointing out that if hundreds of backbenchers were being kept there in the early hours of the morning, ministers could not leave. He still persisted. He was a very important person who had much more urgent things to do than to hang around in Parliament. Why couldn't he go? Finally, the pairing whip exploded. 'Because it's your bloody Bill!' he shouted.

The minister, needless to say, was one of those who had come in on the 'assisted places scheme' and had hardly been seen in the Commons before he was promoted. In fact, he had spent so little time there that the then Deputy Chief Whip commented that they had sent him a map showing the way to the chamber and telling him that the big wooden thing he would find in front of him was the despatch box. Life in Parliament is never fair.

Despite this, there will be some ministers who genuinely do need to be away early, and they are the ones who seldom complain. If they are flying around the world because they are in the Foreign Office, or the Ministries of Defence or International Development, you should help them when you can, especially if the government has a large majority. Flying through different time zones frequently is good for no one's health, and it is not in anyone's interest if they are trying to negotiate on sensitive issues when they are half-asleep. It is certainly not in your party's interests if one of them drops dead from a heart attack, not to mention the fact that it tends to upset their family. Help them out when you can and they will repay your kindness. Well, usually.

The really senior ministers, the ones holding the Great Offices of State, will not be your concern. The Prime Minister, the Chancellor, the Foreign Secretary and the Home Secretary will all have special arrangements made for them by the pairing whip to recognise the special demands made on them. This should not worry you, but if there is grumbling on the back benches that they are never seen, you should pass it on immediately. Having a cup of tea in the tea room or eating in the dining room occasionally is good for them and boosts the morale of their colleagues. It's the job of their Parliamentary Private Secretaries to remind them of this and to make sure that they are not always surrounded by sycophants. Make sure they do.

The greatest crime that a minister can commit, however, is to be late. The reason for this is easy to understand. If a minister is not present in time for the business they are due to speak on, someone else has to do it, and if no one else is there, that job will fall to the government whip. Landing a whip in it like this is the sin against the Holy Ghost for which there is no forgiveness, and you should make sure that no minister in your department ever commits this crime. Ministers who know the House of Commons well and respect it are usually there in plenty of time and may choose to work in their offices in the House beforehand so that they are readily available. They know what you should know, that the timings are always approximate and that the previous business can sometimes finish early. If your department has business on the floor, make sure that the minister dealing with it is there in plenty of time. Ring them and make sure they are in the building, rather than in the department, and, if they are not, insist that they arrive in plenty of time. Don't let the private office put you off with their airy suggestion that there is plenty of time and that the minister is busy. They don't know the House of Commons, and you do (or should). Insist that the minister comes over. Better to have them hanging about than not there when they are needed.

Don't forget the importance of the minister getting to committees on time either. They will start exactly on time whether the minister is there or not. I learnt this the hard way on one of the first committees I ever sat on as a whip. It was a statutory instrument (SI) committee, dealing with a very technical piece of social security legislation, not something on which I have ever pretended to be an expert. Like all new whips, I was nervous. People were slow to arrive but, eventually, all the committee members were there with one important exception

– the minister. I kept looking at my watch and wondering where on earth she was. The minutes ticked away and the chairman reminded me that I would have to move the legislation in her absence. I did not dare leave the room and look for her because if neither of us were present at the right time, the legislation would fall. The clock moved on and the chairman announced the title of the statutory instrument and nodded at me: 'Minister.' Since it was an SI dealing with a technical social security change, this was not something I could just make up as I went along. Slowly and very deliberately, I began to read out the explanatory note that accompanied it. It seemed like the longest few minutes of my life until the minister strolled insouciantly through the door. I got to a suitable stage in the explanation and then said, pointedly, '...which the minister will now explain', and sat down. Far be it from me to name and shame, but Kitty Ussher, you know who you are...

Kitty's remorseful explanation after the committee ended was that she had been outside talking to her officials. I am still unsure how I managed not to explode and remind her that she should have been talking to the committee, but I had wrongly assumed that all ministers understood the need to arrive in plenty of time. Don't make this mistake. Ring them beforehand and check that they will be there, especially if you are dealing with a new minister and, if they are not there, go out and phone them before you get trapped in the room yourself. Finally, make sure that you tell the Deputy Chief Whip so that the erring minister is not given any time off for a few months as a justifiable punishment for the heart attack they nearly induced in you. Whips stick together, and dropping one of their own right in it always results in punishment somewhere along the line. The minister who missed the Third Reading of his own Bill, which I mentioned in the earlier chapter, was never treated with quite the same respect afterwards.

At the opposite end of the spectrum from those who arrive late are the ministers who love making speeches so much that they can never stop talking. Usually this is because they don't understand parliamentary procedure and don't listen when you tell them about it. So, they fail to realise that if a vote is due at the end of the day's main business, say ten or seven o'clock, they must sit down just before then to allow the vote to take place. This time is what is known as 'the moment of interruption', when the main business ends. So, if a vote is not called before then, it won't happen. The government's Bill cannot proceed and you will get the blame. Usually, a quick tug on the back of the jacket is enough to make a minister sit down, and you should make sure that the person sitting next to them knows that they should do it if you give them the nod. Some poor souls fail to respond to this gentle treatment, however, and stronger measures may be necessary. You may offend them, but it is preferable to explaining to the Chief Whip why you have just lost a government Bill.

One minister in the last government, who was a nice man but a little garrulous, had only just been stopped in time on his last outing at the despatch box. The next time he was due to wind up a debate, he found several senior whips sitting behind him, all of whom kept tapping on the shoulders of his Secretary of State, who was sitting next to him, and repeating, 'He does know he's got to sit down before ten?' Even then, we only just got him down in time.

Others require you to adopt even more robust methods. It is not always necessary to go as far as sending an expletive-filled note but, as government whips gather in the chamber when a vote is expected, it is not unusual for half a dozen of them to shout 'sit down' at a minister who shows no sign of finishing a speech. Since they are normally sitting by the Speaker's chair and the minister is at the despatch box, this gentle instruction can usually be heard right across the chamber. The fact that it is never recorded in Hansard is a tribute either to the tact of its reporters, or to the fearsome reputation of the government Whips' Office.

Another tactic is to stand at the bar of the House with your arms folded, looking threatening. You do have to work to perfect the look of quiet menace required on these occasions, but it is worth making the effort. It not only warns the minister that it's time to finish, but lets your backbenchers know that you are on their side in their quest to get home. It is especially useful when the business is something that could be voted on, but a vote is unlikely. In government, you have to keep enough MPs around to win any possible vote but they know, and you know, that they are unlikely to be needed. This often happens on a Thursday afternoon or late at night, and so sensible ministers realise that they will earn the gratitude of their colleagues by being brief. Unfortunately, not all ministers are that sensible, especially when their civil servants have told them that they must get certain things 'on the record'. This is seldom necessary, but civil servants work flexitime and live in London, while most MPs don't. They are not going to get back these wasted hours as time off in lieu and they want to go home to their families, or at least get to bed before midnight. This is one of those few occasions when your colleagues will actually be grateful to you: they may even ask you to go in and tell a long-winded minister to shut up. You should milk it for all that's worth, for it is not often that you encounter gratitude in the course of your work.

If looming around looking menacing doesn't work, you may need to resort to more direct action. One minister was dealing with a piece of business which could have simply been moved formally. It was a Thursday afternoon and the whole of the PLP was waiting to go home. Instead, she decided that this was her moment in the sun and that she would make a speech. A long speech. Naturally, this encouraged members of the opposition, who like nothing better than to keep government MPs hanging around for no useful purpose. They kept trying to make interventions. She kept giving way and answering at length. People were starting to drift off home, depleting our numbers. Prompted by our disgruntled colleagues and by our own desire to get home at a reasonable hour, Tony Cunningham, the pairing whip, and I strolled into the bar of the House and stood, arms folded. I was perfecting my 'any minute, I'm going to lose patience and knife you' look. It didn't work. On and on, she droned. Finally, she took yet another intervention and we cracked. Without any prompting or collusion, both of us yelled loudly across the chamber, 'Oh, for God's sake!' The message had finally got through. She wound up. There wasn't a vote and, after sending out a pager message to tell people they could go, we too headed as fast as possible for the railway station, remembering that it is always better to offend a minister than to explain to the Chief Whip why you have lost a vote.

If ministers can make your life difficult, some former ministers can drive you insane. They are not the majority. Most who lose office accept it with good grace as part of the ups and downs of politics. They enjoyed being a minister while it lasted, but they know that all government jobs are temporary. People like this enjoy being back on the back benches because they have more freedom to pursue the issues that interest them and are no longer stuck on the treadmill of ministerial life. They are generally sane and sensible people who understand that there is more to life than being in government and, since they have always been pleasant to their colleagues, they are welcomed back like long-lost friends. They are valuable as MPs, because they use the expertise they gained in office to good purpose. They know the right questions to ask and they cannot easily be fobbed off. You should respect these people and call on them when you need to. They cannot be manipulated into asking stupid questions or supporting ideas that are clearly flawed, but they will be happy to come to your aid when your party is in a tight corner and they are generally very good at doing so. These are the people you want on your side, and they will be, because they are, first and foremost, party people. Make it clear that you value their experience and expertise and they will often give you valuable advice. After all, we all like to be liked.

Are all ex-ministers like this? Sadly not, for your life would be much easier if they were. Some never get over the trauma of being sacked. While everyone is entitled to a week or two to be resentful and miserable, these people make it a life-long habit. They cannot believe that the government can possibly carry on without them, are sure that they did a good job and that their sacking was unfair. They are certainly wrong in their first assumption. Governments can carry on without anybody. Even if the Prime Minister keeled over, there would be another one along shortly. Realising this should give everyone a sense of perspective, but with some people it never works. They may even be right that their sacking is unfair. People get sacked for all sorts of reason and politics is unfair. Prime Ministers want to bring in fresh faces; there are too many people and not enough jobs. One minister, it is said, lost her job because her name fell off the board when the reshuffle was being worked out and no one realised until there were no jobs left to be filled. There have even been instances of the Downing Street switchboard calling up the wrong person when two people have the same surname. That's life in Westminster.

Yet, instead of taking the advice of one wise ex-minister, who told me that you should be planning your exit from the minute you are appointed, these people think it will never happen to them. They have achieved the office they have wanted all their lives and then convinced themselves that it would go on for ever. They hang around being miserable and feeling victimised, are resentful if you ask them to do any of the jobs that backbenchers normally do, such as serving on committees (indeed, they seem to have forgotten that this is part of an MP's job), and generally make their own and everyone else's lives a misery. The best advice is simply to ignore their moaning and treat them like everyone else. They will eventually accept that they have to do at least some of their share of the work, even if they do it grudgingly. Some will leave Parliament at the next election, believing that it is not worth being there unless you are a minister. Others will hang around, trying to impress new members with their former greatness. There is nothing you can do except to regard them as emotionally damaged and try to be nice to them, however difficult they are. After all, you will eventually be sacked yourself one day.

While the moaners are merely irritating, people who have resigned from the government can be a real pain in the neck. I am not talking about those who go for a genuine reason of conscience, such as their inability to support war in Iraq. They have generally taken their decision after a great deal of thought, even agonising, and they understand the consequences that will follow. People who feel that they have to resign on a big issue like this deserve your sympathy and admiration. The choice they have had to make is not an easy one, for not only are they giving up the ministerial office they have worked hard to obtain, but they are usually party loyalists in every other respect. Indeed, they find it hard precisely *because* they are loyalists. Help them to ease back gently into backbench life by seeking their help when you need it, and never being angry with them. As with many things in politics, you never know whether you will be in that position yourself one day. Of course, there are occasionally those who resign on an issue of conscience with a view to using it for their own advantage later, but these people need not bother you so much. They can be treated in the same way as others who go deliberately to stir up trouble.

These are the ministers who resign out of pique, or to cause problems for the government. Some people decide to go because they believe that the job they have been offered is simply not important enough, or does not reflect their undoubted talents (at least in their own eyes). One minister in the last government resigned because she believed that she should be in the Cabinet and the Prime Minister did not share this view. Nor did most of her colleagues. Others, like Hazel Blears and James Purnell, walk out because they want a change of leader and, no doubt, expect others to follow them. The lesson of history is that it seldom happens but, obviously, they weren't students of history.

Having failed in their aim to precipitate the downfall of a Prime Minister, people like this believe that they are far too important for life on the back benches, even though they have chosen to go there. They expected to start a grand movement, but the fact that they turned out to be leaders without followers in no way diminishes their sense of their own importance. They believe that expecting them to carry out the normal duties of a backbench MP, such as turning up and voting, to be a real imposition. They are far too busy giving interviews to the press about what is wrong with their own government. Since the press feeds their sense of their own importance, it takes them some time to realise that their own party no longer rates them. They may believe they are in the driving seat but, in truth, their troubles are only just beginning. No party likes traitors, and you should remember this when they try to make your life difficult.

Hazel Blears, as is well known, walked out on the day before an election, wearing a badge saying 'Rock the Boat'. Not surprisingly, neither her fellow MPs nor party activists found it at all amusing. Her resignation was announced to the assembled whips at their Wednesday morning breakfast meeting after the Chief had received a telephone call. He had clearly been expecting it and relayed the news briefly and without comment. Some people put their heads in their hands and sighed. Others just muttered, 'Bastards'. Then we got on with the business of the meeting. Nothing is allowed to stop whips doing their jobs, whether it is an economic meltdown or a resigning Cabinet minister, and we found, when we returned to the Commons, that other people were more up to date with developments than we were. They had been sitting watching it all unfold on TV. We had simply been working. You will soon realise that the events that take over the news agenda in the outside world will never take over your day.

When someone has resigned like this, your work is often made easier by the reaction of their colleagues. 'Treacherous' was the word frequently used about Hazel (and, later, about James Purnell) and people's anger was increased because the resignation had clearly been timed to do the maximum damage. MPs were already fighting an uphill battle to try to win votes in the European elections, and they knew that their party workers would be enraged. Hazel's offence was made worse, in the eyes of many people, by the fact that she had been chair of the party and had made a career of presenting herself as a great campaigner and lecturing others on what they should do. Unfortunately, the course did not include a unit entitled 'How Not to Resign the Day before an Election'.

People who behave like this have usually made the fatal error of believing their own publicity. They have continually presented themselves to the press as the great intellectual of the party, or the minister most in touch with the people. Papers recycle what other papers say until this becomes an established 'fact' repeated and enlarged in profiles. Unfortunately, people tend to forget that they started this all off and it feeds their sense of their own self-importance. You do not need to fall into the same trap. Ministers who resign simply to cause problems never have much of a following among their colleagues, who usually believe that anyone lucky enough to make it into the Cabinet ought to have some sense of responsibility. Furthermore, anyone who loses them votes on their own patch is not held in high esteem, which is why, after Hazel walked out, the words 'the day before an election' were repeated frequently, accompanied by either a shaking of the head or a few choice expletives.

When people like this return to the House of Commons, they do not get the welcome they expect and so, although they will make your life difficult, no one will complain if you do the same to them. Therefore, when former ministers refuse to do their share of the work, such as take their turn on committees, you have several options. Some of them will have decided to leave at the next election and will tell you that they are busy looking for a job. Remind them that they already have a job as an elected MP and that it would help if they could do it. If this appeal to their better natures doesn't work, and it seldom does, you should think about their job prospects. Tell them that their chances of getting a well-paid post depend on people believing that they can influence the government and that, if they continue to be awkward, you will ensure that it is made clear that they have no influence whatsoever. They will deny this, of course, and pretend that people will want to employ them for the skills that they have acquired over a lifetime, but they know it's true. Even those who had professional qualifications lose touch after years in Parliament and so their real chance of employment depends on *who* they know, rather than *what* they know. Your threat to damage their chances may not make them cooperative, but it will ensure that they are less uncooperative.

Others may wish to stay on, either because they harbour ambitions for a comeback or because they have nowhere else to go. Some will simply ignore your calls when you want to check that they will attend a committee or be at an important vote, or they will demand personal notification whenever you require their presence. One ex-minister told me that I had not requested his presence when I enquired why he had missed a vote. I told him that he received a document each week called the whip and that three lines on it meant that he was required to turn up. MPs do not receive personal invitations to vote for their own government.

'If you're going to be like that, I won't turn up at all,' was the response.

'Fine,' I told him. 'We can deal with that.'

I meant that the whips would take great delight in starting off the procedure that would result in the whip being removed from him, meaning he would no longer be a member of the parliamentary party. Sadly, before we could do this, he announced that he was leaving Parliament and later got a very well-paid job at the BBC. It is rumoured that the Beeb believed that he would be great at influencing a future Labour government. As one of my colleagues said, 'Dream on.'

You should also be able to judge how precarious a person's position in their own constituency is. While one ex-minister boasted to her friends that she was 'giving the whips the run around', it was obvious that she was in so much trouble on her own patch that she would not dare miss a key vote. In such circumstances, the best response is sarcasm. Make sure that you wait for people like this in the lobby and make it clear that you know they have no choice but to turn up. Be effusively and sarcastically grateful while enquiring how things are going in the constituency.

Others may not be in so much trouble back home (although they won't be finding rose petals strewn at their feet) and therefore feel that they can be as awkward and obstructive as possible. There are several ways of dealing with this. Former ministers who refuse to do the work that they expected others to do for them when they were in office are never popular, so you should make sure that everyone else knows what they are up to. This tactic works particularly well when they are refusing to do statutory instrument committees. These are mind-numbingly boring pieces of secondary legislation and most MPs hate them. That is why people are allocated to them on a rota basis, so that everyone, in theory at least, does their fair share. If a former minister is refusing to turn up, get their colleagues to make loud remarks in the tea room about the loyalty they expected when in office and how their attitude has suddenly changed. Encourage them to complain, in the offending minister's hearing, that they are having to do too many committees because some people are not pulling their weight. This usually gives anyone plotting a comeback pause for thought but, if it doesn't work, you may have to unleash the ultimate deterrent: deny them offices.

Office space is tight in the House of Commons and nice offices are hard to find. Many MPs still work in tiny, windowless rooms without any natural daylight. Getting a decent office is often considered the pinnacle of achievement and ex-ministers feel they are entitled to the best. Generally, those serving in government do not have good offices in the House because they spend most of their time over in their department. When they return to the back benches, even if they have resigned of their own accord, they expect accommodation that befits what they consider to be their status.

This usually takes some time to arrange as a lot of people have to move around following a reshuffle and those lucky few who have nice offices understandably do not wish to give them up. So, if ex-ministers are being awkward, you should see the accommodation whip (yes, there is one) and make sure he delays finding them a new office for as long as possible. When compelled to find something, he can then offer one of the tiny cubicles on the upper committee corridor which have no windows. Your awkward ex-minister will be outraged at this insult to their dignity and complain. Tell him or her that they don't really need an office as they aren't turning up to do their job. Remember to stand well back as you do this, since these are very important people who need their status confirmed every day. They will be outraged. After the explosion, you can say that you will speak to the accommodation whip, but only if they agree to stop messing you about. This works with a lot of people, who accept that they have got to the end of the road. For those who remain intransigent, you have one final card to play. You can find out when they have been allocated an office and have accepted it, and then go to the Chief Whip and tell him that this person is refusing to do any work. When I did this, he picked up the phone and said simply, 'You know those office moves I authorised the other day? Cancel them please.' Job done.

This whole process will take some time, but remember that it is a war of attrition. The people you are dealing with are being interviewed by the press regularly. They appear on television, commenting on what the government is doing wrong.

Consequently, they feel that they are very important and that the country is hanging on their every word. The important thing to remember is that they are no longer on your side. They are out to cause the maximum damage to the government, which it is your job to serve. Most of your backbenchers understand this and believe that these people are doing their best to lose them their seats. Since no one is keen on people who want to put them on the dole, especially when they know that those same people are likely to get well-paid jobs, they will not mind you giving them a hard time. In fact, they will enjoy it. So, cheer up your troops by making it clear that you think these people are totally unimportant. Eventually, even the most awkward former minister will get the message. There is nothing so 'ex' as an ex-minister. A dog may be obeyed in office but, once the office is gone, people realise that he's just a dog.

Chapter 7

How to deal with
the civil service

I T I S A N inescapable fact that being attached to a department means having to deal with civil servants. No doubt all of these people are shining examples of intellectual brilliance; the people who brought us Blue Streak, Concorde and the NHS computer system.

Unfortunately, these intellectual giants know nothing about how Parliament works. The only ones who do are working in the Whips' Office. Departmental civil servants will consider your repeated insistence that their ministers are around to vote to be an unwarranted interruption in the smooth running of the department, and they see no reason why Members of the government should have to waste time putting the government's legislation on the statute book. They like ministers who follow the department's timetable, agree with the civil servants running it, and do as they're told.

Your first job as a whip is to make it clear that you are not a soft touch and that your job is to win votes for the government. Begin by talking to the diary secretaries in your department. These are usually women on the lowest rung of the private office ladder and poorly paid. Be nice to them because they are not your problem. When they appear to be getting in the way of government business, remember that they are carrying out instructions from elsewhere.

You should explain to them exactly what your job is and how you want to deal with requests for ministerial absences. Don't assume that they know all this as it's quite probable that no one has bothered to explain it to them before. It's sensible to make it clear at the start that you want all requests on your desk (or sent by email if you prefer) by a certain time each week, and that you will only deal with them at that time. Decide the day and the time depending on when your pairing whip wants to deal with absence requests for the following week and explain that he or she has lots of requests to deal with and can only allow a certain number of people to be away. Make it clear that all requests go from you to the pairing whip and you will let them know as soon as a decision is made. See that you stick to that promise, because it will help the diary secretaries, but explain that you have other work to do and that you cannot be constantly on call to deal with absence requests. You will save yourself a lot of aggravation by being clear about this at the start and not expecting people to read your mind.

If you really want to get the diary secretaries on-side, ask them over for tea in the House of Commons. Unlike senior civil servants, they don't get the chance to come over there and they will love it if you show them around. Take them into the Whips' Office so that they can see how you work (and understand that you do not have a host of staff at your disposal) and make them feel part of what you're doing. Introduce them to the Chief Whip if he or she is around and not too busy. If that's not possible, get the Deputy to make a fuss of them. Show them that you appreciate that they are under pressure trying to fit lots of appointments into a crowded diary and they will be much more disposed to be helpful to you. However, you should remember that they are often under pressure from those above them who will be insisting that a minister fulfils an engagement when you want him back to vote. Don't expect them to take on their bosses. That's your job.

The civil service operates by keeping ministers busy so that they have little time to think. It mistakes activity for achievement and only very confident ministers are able to buck the system. In fact, the first rule for any minister should be to get control of the diary, but I have known few who manage to do this. One insisted that nothing was put in without his approval, others that they would eat in the members' dining room on a certain night each week, or that papers should be brought to them for a decision during the day instead of being placed in their boxes for them to work on late at night. All of these small victories were gained after long battles, and so many ministers don't even try. They are too afraid of being labelled lazy by the Whitehall machine and of that judgement being fed back to Downing Street. In insisting that they come to the House of Commons, therefore, you will be saving them from themselves, even though some of them may not see it that way.

Each week, you will receive a list of requests for ministers in the department to be absent on certain days, or at certain times, to carry out ministerial duties. Before you pass these to the pairing whip for a final decision, make sure that you have checked them thoroughly and that all the necessary information is there. If you don't do this, the pairing whip will send them back to you asking for more information, so save yourself time and effort by getting it right the first time. You will want to know the purpose of each engagement, the exact amount of time it will take and when the minister will be back. Some of the requests will be for important things that a minister needs to do. In such cases, you should do your best to assist them with time off because you are there to help them do their job. Others will be for things that are totally unimportant politically but that, for some reason, the department considers essential. Sending ministers off on visits to seats your party will win only when hell freezes over, insisting he talks to a conference of the National Society of Hole Punch Collectors or that he meets a delegation from the Society for the Preservation of Glass Bottles should never rate highly on your scale of priorities.

In these cases, it's wise to ring the minister concerned to find out if there is a good reason for these seemingly pointless activities. Ring him on his mobile rather than going through the private office, remembering that the civil servants listen in to landline calls. Even better, catch him in the lobby. You will often find that he knows nothing about the dubious engagement in his diary or, if he does, is anxious to get rid of it. Amazing though it is, some ministers cannot give instructions or stand up to their civil servants and would much rather that you did it for them. It is much easier to blame the nasty Whips' Office for your inability to fulfil an engagement than to tell your private office that it's a complete waste of your time. You should save these poor creatures from themselves by forbidding them to miss a vote. They will thank you for it.

If you discover that the minister really *does* want to go off and do something useless, then appeal to his better nature ('this is a very important vote') or to his desire to stay in government ('the Prime Minister is really interested in this and wants to see it go through'). The approach you choose will depend upon the person you are dealing with. Party loyalists usually respond best to the first approach and careerists to the second, but you would be unwise to try it with anyone who knows the Prime Minister better than you do. You do not want to elicit a reply telling you that he is not interested at all and that he has never mentioned this legislation in his many private chats with the minister.

Very occasionally, because even whips can be wrong sometimes, you will find that the minister has a good reason for doing the engagements that you have dismissed as useless. If it is a good political reason, then you should help out and try to get the time off approved. You can always blame the pairing whip if you don't succeed. If the reason is not so good, and he has simply promised a visit to someone he once met at a conference or some other daft excuse, then tell him to back out. Your job is to save the government, not his face. The only time you should help with these sorts of engagements (that a minister has taken on because he can't say no) is when you are not really worried about winning a vote and you want the minister to owe you a favour. On these occasions, you should make it very clear that it will be extremely hard to persuade the pairing whip to approve his absence but that you will do your level best and take the flak for him. Make it clear that you are only doing this to avoid him being embarrassed. Any half-decent person will realise that they owe you and the debt can be repaid by staying late when they are needed or, if you have really pulled out all the stops, by a visit to your constituency. Be warned, however, that not all ministers are half-decent people and some will not recognise the obligation they are under at all. Learn your lesson and save your retaliation for another time.

You should look especially closely at any engagement scheduled for a Thursday. Some ministers like their department to arrange Thursday visits which, by a happy coincidence, always end near their homes. They can then get home early while backbenchers are still stuck in Westminster. This is an entirely human aspiration, but not one you should indulge.

If these engagements start turning up in the diary on a regular basis, you need to discuss it with the pairing whip, who will be as anxious as you are to put a stop to this practice. It may make the minister's life easier, but it will make things harder for the whips. Backbenchers who are being kept away from their loved ones, or, at least, their families, will be furious. If they find themselves regularly walking through the lobbies on Thursday when many ministers are absent, they will become mutinous and more inclined than usual to try to slope off early in the hope that there won't be a vote. No one needs that kind of problem.

The difficulty you will face is that, even if you talk to a minister about his engagements, there is always some floppy-haired Rupert in the private office who will try to get things put back into the diary after you have agreed they should be taken out. This man (and it usually is a man) is destined to become a Permanent Secretary in the future – and he knows it. He works through order and hierarchy. He believes that there has to be a system for checking and re-checking everything and that no one ever takes a real decision because he has never had to take one on his own. He will use up hours of your time unless you deal with him firmly right at the start.

When you refuse to allow a minister time off, Rupert will adopt a number of strategies. His first will be to tell you how important the engagement is. Tell him that it may be important to him, but it is of not the slightest importance to the government. He will undoubtedly refer to the vital importance of the minister addressing the conference of ball-bearing manufacturers or whatever it is he has put in the diary. It is vital, he will tell you, that the minister meets these people. Respond by telling him that it is vital the government wins votes in the House of Commons.

His next approach will be to imply that you are a mere junior clerk who knows nothing at all about the workings of government and should not be dealing with these vital issues. Remind him that you are a minister in Her Majesty's Government, doing a job the Prime Minister has asked you to do. If he is really obnoxious, you can insist that he addresses you as 'minister' to hammer home that fact. Tell him that he may be ringing on behalf of a department, but you are ringing on behalf of the Prime Minister, and his minister is required in the House.

This approach works with most people and it is best to remain calm but firm. You are acting on behalf of the government and he is not. Do not enter into negotiations. You are simply re-iterating a decision that has been made by the whips. Being a civil servant, he will then try to find out what the appeals process is, because the civil service is a vast bureaucracy that avoids decisions by constantly reviewing them. It is unwise to try sarcasm at this point because he probably won't recognise it. Just tell him that there is no appeal, the decision has been taken and that's it. I once unwisely told a civil servant that he could appeal to the Chief Whip, but that he would tell him exactly what I had told him, the only difference being that he would be cross at being disturbed. The man I had spoken to did not take the hint and rang the Chief anyway. He did and he was. Another colleague once told a diary secretary who asked about appeals that there was a person in the office she could ring. His name, he said, was Tommy McAvoy and he was always patient and willing to listen. Tommy, later the Deputy Chief Whip, was, at that time, the long-serving pairing whip and notoriously hard to persuade to let anyone have time off. She was just writing down his name when a more experienced diary secretary intervened. 'Don't go there,' she warned.

If you become a more senior whip, you will find that calls are often referred to you either by junior whips who have encountered someone very difficult, or by the civil servants in the back office who are often bombarded by calls from departments. The absolute rule is that you always support your colleagues, even if their decision is wrong. You can gently point this out to them afterwards but you should never, ever allow departmental civil servants to believe that they can persuade you to overrule another whip. Whips stand or fall together and mistakes are dealt with inside the office and never discussed with outsiders. Furthermore, if you allow such a belief to get about, you will be inundated with calls and never be able to get on with your proper job. If someone is being really difficult, icy disdain is the best approach ('I understand that the departmental whip has already told you this. Why have you come through to me?'). Tell them that you do not have time to waste repeating something that they have already been told and that you expect them to listen to what their whip tells them in the future. In the worst cases, try being carefully rude. I once asked someone 'Which bit of the word "no" are you having a problem with?' He didn't try that tactic again. What you should not ever do is lose your temper, or even raise your voice. You are in the driving seat here. If someone keeps arguing with you, simply tell them that the decision is made, you have got work to get on with and you cannot spend any more time on their call.

Departments that ring up the whips' assistants are usually either querying a decision, and hoping that they will get more sympathy from fellow civil servants, or wanting to know what time the votes will be. This happens when there is a running three-line whip and votes could come at any time. Do not, on any account, give them even an approximate time for the vote. They will take it as certain and, if the vote comes early, the minister may miss it. You will then get into trouble as well as him. Just say that you don't know. They will, no doubt, tell you that they need to know because the minister has very important meetings that afternoon, so suggest the minister moves his meetings to his House of Commons office. Civil servants hate the idea of doing this because it means that they have to move across as well, but it is the most sensible solution on such a day. Do not do what one whip did and tell them that the timing of votes on these occasions is in the hands of the opposition and not the government (even though it's true). 'Shall I ring them then?' the bright voice at the other end of the line asked.

Dealing with your department does not only mean a battle over time off. You will also need to find out what they are hiding from you. Since civil servants usually fail to recognise that whips are government ministers, many of them will treat you as the lowest of the low and refuse to tell you anything. Sometimes, of course, this attitude is determined by the Secretary of State, but most of the time it is the result of their failure to understand either Parliament or what you do. Since the things they are hiding usually turn out to be the things that will cause most trouble for the government, then you have to insist on your rights. Make sure that they invite you to departmental meetings and insist that they tell you if the time of the meeting is changed, as some departments have an unfortunate habit of forgetting to do this. Make a fuss if necessary. If the Deputy Chief Whip needs to call someone senior in the department and insist that you are involved, then ask him to do it. When you do attend meetings, make sure that you are part of the discussion and that you sit with the ministers in the department. When I first went to a meeting at the Ministry of Justice, I found that I had been placed low down the table with the Spads. I moved my nameplate and it didn't happen again.

You may find that if you join a department that is mid-way through preparing a Bill, everyone will discuss the proposed legislation as if you already know about it. This is simply an attempt to exclude you from the discussion, which you should not tolerate. Ask questions if people are talking in jargon, make sure that the civil servant in charge of the Bill team talks you through it and spend time making sure that you understand what is being proposed and have thought through its political ramifications. If there is anything likely to cause trouble with your own side, then you must be aware of it from the start. Civil servants generally adhere to the fond belief that their 'handling strategy', which they draw up for each Bill, will deal with any problems. It won't. Their strategy usually involves briefing the opposition spokespersons, chairs of the relevant select committees and anyone who has shown an interest in this kind of legislation. They are not there to deal with malcontents on your own back benches and will have no idea who they are. That is where you come in.

Remember, though, that you are not there to change policy. Of course you will have a view (you would not be a politician if you didn't), although a few seem to manage the process without any views of their own at all. Sadly, your opinion is not important. Your job is to get that piece of legislation through Parliament even if you think it is completely barmy. If you are not prepared for that, you shouldn't have joined the Whips' Office. Not being able to express a view on policy (except within the confines of the office) is the reason that whips are often not assigned to areas about which they know a lot. When I was appointed, I was told that I could not possibly go the Department for Children, Schools and Families because I 'knew too much about it'. The assumption was that I would not be able to restrain myself if I thought a policy was wrong and that, not being a meek and mild soul and knowing a bit about it, I might be tempted argue my corner. This was probably true. Besides, I was needed to keep an eye on departments that might cause problems, and Children, Schools and Families was not one of them.

While you are not there to argue about policy, you do not need to share the blithe assumption of civil servants, and some ministers, that, as they obviously know what is best for the country, everyone will fall in behind what they have agreed. MPs are used to being argumentative. While civil servants think that meetings will overcome any opposition and many ministers are convinced that their powers of eloquence will persuade doubters to come on board, it is your job to see the elephant traps for what they are – a great big hole that the government will fall into if you do not get it stopped.

So, when you come across something that you know will have your own MPs frothing at the mouth and demanding blood, you should sound the alarm immediately. Alert the Chief Whip or his Deputy. It isn't your job to argue any damaging propositions out of the Bill, but it is your job to let your bosses know that they are on their way. It's then the job of the Chief Whip to discuss them with the Secretary of State and, if necessary, the Prime Minister, especially if he thinks there is something coming up that will cause a row on his own side or that he may not get through the House and might lead to a government defeat. 'It's the Chief Whip's job', a wise former MP once told me, 'to tell the Prime Minister things he doesn't want to hear.' You aren't paid enough to tell even a Secretary of State that, so steer clear. You have done your job by alerting those above you.

One example of when this happened was the proposal to allow the police to hold terrorist suspects for up to forty-two days. The Bill had only just got through the Commons on its Second Reading and was being mangled in the Lords. The Chief Whip believed that he would not be able to keep enough of our own side (and certainly not the DUP, who had voted with us) around for the time it would take to engage in the end-of-session 'ping-pong' with the Lords. People would simply disappear and we might lose. Somehow, he persuaded the Prime Minister of this, and Jacqui Smith was forced to come to the House and make a humiliating climb-down, withdrawing the Bill. What he had said to achieve this he never revealed. His conversations with the Prime Minister remained private even from other whips. It cannot have been an easy conversation, but it saved the government from a defeat.

Chapter 8

What everyone wants

THERE ARE ALWAYS people who want something from MPs and this is even more true if you become a whip. At the first Labour Party conference I attended after the 1997 election, people I hardly recognised came up to me and hugged me or patted me on the shoulder, telling me how glad they were that I'd been elected and that they'd always known I'd make it into Parliament. Each of them went on to confide their own ambition to be an MP and to ask for my advice. My real friends had sent their congratulations a long time before.

This combination of crawling and flattery will assail you even more when you are made a whip. Some of it will come from

MPs, who want to get promoted or to be allowed home regularly, some of it will come from within the party from people who think you have influence, and some will be from well-meaning but ignorant folk outside politics who think you can control the government legislation. How wrong they are!

Have no truck with any of this. Once you start to play favourites with people, you will have no credibility as a whip. As I've explained, the only people you might, occasionally, do a favour for are your close friends and, even then, you have to be sure that you won't get them, or yourself, into trouble. Nevertheless, you will have to deal with these people firmly, because they will plague you all the time if you don't start off in the right way. Don't shrink from it. Before you decide how to do this it is as well to be aware of the different categories of people who will want something from you.

1. The self-important

There are some people in Parliament who really do need to be let off votes to do important things. You cannot take the Prime Minister away from a meeting of world leaders, bring the Chancellor back from a financial summit, or drag the Foreign Secretary half-way around the world unless the government really does face losing an important vote. This will then be communicated to them by the Chief Whip, who is paid to do such things.

Your problem is not people who are important, but, rather, those who think they are important. Some of them will love giving speeches (or 'lectures', if they really want to sound good) to think tanks, charities, lobby groups and all sorts of other London-based parasites who *also* like to think they are important and influence the political process. The people prepared to go and talk to them are labelled as 'thinkers' or 'intellectuals', often prefaced with the word 'leading'. They then get invitations to address more and more groups as a result of that designation. After all, that must be true because it's in the papers.

In the end, the MPs caught up on this carousel ride of speech, publicity, 'intellectual' status and more invitations to give speeches, can stop doing real politics altogether and, if they really work at it, become one of your party's 'leading theoreticians'. The problem is that they think it is much more important to be out giving lectures on politics than actually voting to implement some government policies, so they will want to be let off all the time. They will tell you how important these engagements are, so tell them that what is important is winning votes. Their next argument will be that they are helping to develop policy or 'laying the ground' for a future election victory. In this case, you can suggest that if they really want to do that, talking to some people outside the small world of London SW1 might help, and offer to arrange for them to visit a marginal seat and talk to some real voters. If you wish to be really difficult, suggest they help the local candidate to arrange a meeting where some of these ideas can be discussed with local people. You need have no fear that they will really do this, since all their activity is a voter-avoidance strategy.

They will, of course, accuse you of being a thuggish whip who just wants to stifle debate. Tell them they have plenty of time for debate on Fridays, Saturdays and Sundays. On Mondays to Thursdays, you expect them to be voting for the government.

They will then go above your head and appeal to the Chief Whip or the Deputy Chief Whip, who are likely to be as unsympathetic as you are, since these people believe that others are there to do the donkey work while they are around to give intellectual guidance. You might want to have a word beforehand to make sure that they get told that the best use for their stellar brains is in the chamber – or you may not, knowing that they're either hopeless when challenged by the other side or very boring to your own. Whatever you do, stand firm. Once you give in to these people and accept them at their own valuation, then you will never get them back into good voting habits.

The second category of the self-important consists of people who believe that nothing, absolutely nothing, can take place in the constituency without them being present. These people have no discrimination. Whether the event is a vicarage tea party or the opening of a new roundabout, they have to be there. (Yes, I do know someone who opened a roundabout!) They have failed to even try to get their constituents to understand that they're in London during the week, accept every engagement without discrimination, and believe it will be a catastrophe if they do not go.

Some of these poor souls are desperately insecure and convinced that they will lose their seats if they don't go to absolutely everything, and this insecurity is usually totally unrelated to the size of their majority. Others believe that they are so essential to the daily life of Anytown that nothing can go on without them. You need to break it to them gently that it can.

People with genuinely marginal seats need to be away more than others, but you can only meet their needs if you do not let others go unnecessarily. All of the self-important people will, when they've run out of other excuses, beg you to let them go as a favour. They will flatter you by telling you that, while others don't understand the importance of their requests, you do. They will promise you favours in return, such as speaking on a difficult Bill, or being on a committee you need to fill. Don't believe them and don't give in or they will be back with another request next week. Your job is to keep a majority there for the government and, if you can, let MPs with marginal seats attend important engagements. You are not there to pander to people's egos or to be their best friend. You're a whip and these people are not going to like you. Get used to it.

2. The forgetful

It's amazing how forgetful some MPs can be. They forget when Parliament is sitting. They forget that they should only book holidays or important events in the recess and then they will come to you to ask you, as a favour, to honour their arrangements.

Sometimes, you may be able to. If it's only the last day they want to miss, you know there is not going to be much happening and they know it too.

People who ask for this are usually old hands who know the score and know that it's easy for you to let them go. Don't try to fool them that there might be an important vote or you will just look an idiot. Give them a nod and a wink and they'll pay you back in the future by doing you a favour. They've been around long enough to know how the place works.

Others will claim to have got the dates wrong when you know full well that they're leaving early because it's cheaper. Resign yourself to the fact that they're going to go anyway. Most MPs are not as well-off as people think and a holiday is an expensive item. The insurance won't cover them if their excuse is 'the whips wouldn't let me go', so there is no chance that they will cancel. Their families are looking forward to it and there's nothing you can do, so resign yourself to the inevitable and make the best of it. Say you will speak to the pairing whip and get them paired. You will probably be able to do this because the other side will have the same problem and they, too, will know there's nothing to be done.

Get your revenge later. Put these people on the most boring committees you can find, select them for statutory instruments that will run for the full hour and a half. Don't let them have the new office they want. This is petty and spiteful, but you are allowed to do it because you're a whip. There aren't many consolations in the job, so take them when you can and enjoy them. The poor sap on the receiving end may not even make the link between what's happening to them and their previous behaviour, but you will know.

3. The religious

There are, the public might be surprised to learn, some genuinely religious people in Parliament, and many of them do not make a show of their faith.

You will see Catholics appearing on Ash Wednesday with smudges of ash on their foreheads, which makes them fairly easy to recognise. There are some who follow the Evangelical path and even some genuinely religious people who belong to the Church of England.

All of those are relatively easy to cope with. The chapel in the undercroft holds regular Church of England and Catholic services on the main holy days (that's where the ashes come from). People will sometimes be invited to Lambeth Palace for Christmas carols or to Westminster Cathedral for the installation of a new cardinal. There will be people there from all parties (although you won't find many Ulster Unionists greeting a new cardinal), so it's easy to arrange with opposition whips that you will pair them and not call them back for a vote. MPs rushing out of church when their phones bleep do not do much for the reputation of Parliament.

The main events for other faiths will not fall neatly around a parliamentary calendar, which arranges holidays for Christmas and Easter, so you will need to make special arrangements for them. In my experience, people do not come demanding time off but are instead rather sheepish about it. A friend once confided, very quietly, that she was going home for Yom Kippur. 'Well, of course you are,' was my reply.

As I once told a meeting, I'm prepared to do most things for the Labour Party, but I wouldn't change my religion for it. Nor do I expect anyone else to do so.

If someone needs to be away for Eid, Yom Kippur, or any other religious event, you should arrange it for them. Opposition whips will be quite accommodating as they will often have people who need to be away too. Even if they haven't, they will recognise the need to accommodate these things in a diverse society. This does not mean that you need feel obligated to supply pairs so that their people can go to the Bullingdon Club reunion. Whatever some might think, this does not yet count as a religious festival.

You should also be sensitive (yes, even though you are a whip) to people's religious beliefs. Do not encourage colleagues to heckle people expressing fundamentalist beliefs on issues they regard as a matter of faith, even if you think they are mad. They are entitled to their point of view and Parliament is a debating chamber. Indeed, matters like gay marriage, abortion and so on should not be whipped anyway, even though leaders sometimes like to try. Trying to whip the votes on gay marriage caused endless trouble for the Labour leadership and alienated people were happy to vote for the principles of the Bill, but wished to see some amendments.

You will also find that colleagues don't necessarily want to draw attention to what they are doing. There are a surprising number of Catholic MPs who still give up something for Lent, usually alcohol or chocolate. This is not a practice they wish to advertise, so do not wave glasses of wine or KitKats under their noses – unless they are your friends, in which case you can tease them as much as you like.

Muslim colleagues may be fasting during Ramadan, which is particularly hard if it falls during a northern summer. They will have not eaten or drunk since before sunrise, so try to help them out. Don't put them on committees during the afternoons, so they have a chance for a lie down. If someone is a frontbencher and has business in front of the House, especially if it is a Report Stage with amendments to a Bill, you might gently suggest to one of their colleagues that they take over some of the work to give them a break. You would hope that the team has already thought about this, but don't bank on it. Do all this quietly and don't make a fuss. Not only is it the right and proper thing to do, but people will feel an obligation to you as a result. A whip managing to do the right thing and having someone owe them a favour is a rare combination and one to be savoured.

4. The charities

Many charities employ highly paid people to advise them on how Parliament works. Unfortunately, most of these people don't have a clue about what actually goes on there. They are the bane of an MP's life because, to try to justify their high salaries, they organise useless campaigns that only use up a lot of their time. These are the people who organise email campaigns demanding that you sign a particular Early Day Motion, even if you are on the front bench and so can't sign them. They get hundreds of people to write to you, clogging up your email, even though most of these people don't know what an Early Day Motion is and aren't aware that it accomplishes nothing. They involved your staff in preparing hundreds of letters in response and you signing them all. They are also the people who will email asking you to write to a minister demanding he does something, even if the minister is not one of your own side and so will not take any notice whatsoever of your opinion, or even see your letter. This is doubly true if the minister is on your side.

Your problem is that the people writing to you are usually decent, well-intentioned souls who have been misled about how the system actually works because the people organising campaigns don't understand it. Be warned that the problems get worse if you are a whip.

People outside assume that you have some power over legislation. You don't want to explain that you have no influence whatsoever (apart from saying in a whips' meeting that you cannot get some minister's stupid bloody idea through), so you need to let them down gently.

If you are the whip on a Bill that charities have an interest in, they will try to lobby you. Do not, on any account, meet them. That is not your job and, if you are sympathetic, you may be drawn into making promises you can't keep, or they will think you have made promises when you haven't. People hear what they want to hear, generally. Ignore the emails and letters. If they catch you on the phone, say gently that this is not something a whip can engage in and then shut up.

You will be in real trouble if the minister thinks you are trying to change his policy. Let them lobby members of the Bill committee by all means, let them seek meetings with ministers, but do not get involved yourself.

If you are a Lord Commissioner of Her Majesty's Treasury (or, in normal parlance, a slightly more senior whip), there are people, and these campaigners are among them, who will think you have some influence on the Treasury. I was once wrongly listed as a Lord Commissioner and only realised when letters were forwarded on to me from the Treasury asking me to lobby the Chancellor for more overseas aid. Do not go there. It is way above your pay grade. If people from the constituency write to you, just send a nice letter back explaining that this is not your role. If the letters are from anyone else, ignore them. Trying to tell the Chancellor, any Chancellor, what his policies should be will do nothing for your future career prospects.

If you are unlucky enough to be in charge of a Bill when the general election is called, you will have even more problems. You would assume that people who work as Parliamentary Liaison Officers or anything similar might understand what happens at the end of a parliament, but this assumption would be wrong. What actually happens is that Bills, or parts of Bills, which are agreed by both sides, go through. Others, which would require a fight, are dropped. This process is known as 'wash up' and it happens because MPs are rushing off to start the election campaign. Only those in safe seats, or those who are retiring, or poor sods like whips, who have to be there, stay to the very end.

Nevertheless, when I was seeing the Bribery Bill through

its passage at the end of a parliament, I started to receive emails and letters asking me to ensure that the government put the Bill on the statute book. We did, but not because of the campaign. The Bill went through because the Tories didn't want to be seen as being in favour of bribery. Who would? It was all agreed, so it would pass.

Eventually, I phoned one of the charities involved (which happened to be one I knew well), explained what was going on and asked them if they would kindly stop all the emails. I still don't think they believed me.

If you have to deal with a Bill which is being drastically cut or abandoned, you will not have the chance to smooth things over. It will be your fault, even though these things are agreed between the two Chief Whips (Liberal Democrats don't count for these purposes). You can write to people and explain how and why things are done like this but they are unlikely to believe you. Take it on the chin. You should be used to getting the blame by now.

5. Constituents

Constituents get favours, right? There is an obvious reason: they can vote for you. No one else can and you need to remember that.

If your constituency is a long way from London, you will not get many visitors, but be nice to them when they do arrive. Follow Paul Flynn's advice and do not act as a tour guide unless you want to give the impression that you have nothing else to do, but book them on a tour of the House and try to meet them afterwards if you can.

Sometimes, you may want to take them for a cup of tea, but restrict the refreshments to non-alcoholic ones unless you want people to believe that you spend all your time in the bar. At other times, a quick few minutes' catch up to find out how they've enjoyed the tour will do. At that point, you may want to show them a quick glimpse of your place of work, the fabled government Whips' Office, just so they can see how basic and uncomfortable it is. You do not want them to go home thinking that you live in luxury.

Stick your head around the door and ask your colleagues first so that they can stop any slanderous conversations they are having about ministers. Then, a quick look around, with you pointing at your own desk, where the Deputy sits and where the Chief's office is, will be enough. Constituents will go home happy since they have seen something which is not on the standard tour and they will tell other people that they are happy. Job done!

Many visitors to Parliament want to see Prime Minister's Questions and they are not satisfied with substitutes. While people complain loudly about the standards of behaviour at PMQs, they are singularly reluctant to accept tickets for anything else on the grounds that other question times are boring. They will tend to believe that you have special access to PMQ tickets. Disabuse them of this idea immediately and explain that, like everyone else, you get two tickets occasionally, allocated on a rota basis.

If there are some particularly faithful supporters coming up from Anytown, you might try to scrounge tickets from someone else, and whips are usually happy to give their unused tickets to other whips. If you obtain some, you should make it clear that you have gone through hell and sold your soul to the devil in order to obtain them, but you have done so because of your high regard for these visitors from home. In a sense, this is true. Doing a favour for another whip is part of a Faustian Pact. Whoever has given them to you will expect a favour back one day.

You will need to get your visitors a copy of the Order Paper and explain how it works, otherwise they will not understand why they have this list of names in front of them but people are bobbing up and down dementedly and others, who are not listed, are being allowed to ask questions. Then take them to where they have to wait and ask a friendly doorkeeper to keep an eye on them and send them in the right direction. Explain that you cannot escort them in because you have to be present at PMQs. You need not explain that your job is to encourage your own side to cheer the Prime Minister and to barrack the Leader of the Opposition, but tell them where you will be sitting so that they can find you. People like to know where you are; after all, they put you there.

Chapter 9

How to find your information

ONCE YOU BECOME a whip, lots of people will be reluctant to talk to you. You are part of what the PLP fondly refers to as 'the Stasi'. They think that you are spying on them and, in some ways, you are. You need information, to know what people are thinking. Without this, you cannot do your job.

Paradoxically, the people who most want to talk to you are the ones you should ignore. There are ignoble people in politics who love to rat on their colleagues because they believe that it will help their own advancement. They are the same people who are all too ready to give anonymous comments to the press whenever someone is in trouble, or who like to get up and denounce any so-called abuse that some passing journalist has called to their attention, even if it hasn't actually happened. These people are those that MPs categorise as 'whips' narks' and you should place no reliance on anything they tell you. They are the lowest of the low.

Firstly, their information is likely to be inaccurate and informed by their own prejudices, but, also, they are usually poor saps who feel the need to trash other people's reputations because they cannot rely on their own ability to get them where they want to be. Most whips despise people like that and, although some will use them occasionally, giving them an awkward question to put forward in the Chamber or asking them to stand up on an issue that no one else wants to be associated with, they never recommend them for promotion. If they are so obviously untrustworthy and easily manipulated, would you really want to put them in a minister's chair? Moreover, since these people demonstrate daily that they care about nothing except their own advancement, why would anyone trust them?

Nevertheless, these people still slime their way around the House of Commons looking for a willing ear into which they can pour their thoughts. You may sometimes be unable to avoid them, but you should never take them seriously. If you feel like a bit of entertainment, it can be worth starting a rumour and directing it towards them so that they end up coming to tell you about your own invented piece of gossip. Then, when they approach you to tell you X is in financial trouble or Y is seeing a young secretary, you can shake your head, look very knowing but mysterious, and say, 'Oh no, you've got the wrong person there. It's someone entirely different.' They will then waste days trying to find out who is really in trouble and annoy most of their colleagues in the process. It's a just retribution for their behaviour.

Yet, information is your currency and so you do want people to feel able to talk to you. They will only do this if you have followed the advice on dealing with your colleagues and they know that you will not be trying to get them into trouble if they say one word that is critical of the government. Just as it is the Chief Whip's job to tell the Prime Minister things he doesn't want to hear, so it is your job to listen to things you may not want to hear, otherwise you will not know if people are discontented. They might just feel generally overlooked and ignored, in which case your job is to lend a friendly ear and convince them that they are trusted and valued members of the parliamentary party. The person you are speaking to may be a crashing bore but they are *your* crashing bore and if you want them to go through the lobbies night after night, supporting the government when it is in trouble, then the least you can do is give them a bit of your time.

Other people will want to tell you why they don't like a certain piece of legislation, or why they believe that the party is going in the wrong direction. It is your job to listen to them and make sure that the Chief is aware if there is a groundswell of discontent. Ministers never like to admit it, but sometimes their backbench colleagues are right and may be more in tune with the public mood than they are. On the other hand, they may be just a bunch of grumbling miseries. However, a whole lot of grumbling miseries can still cause real problems for the party, even when they are wrong. Others will know more about the subject than the minister does and a sensible minister will listen to these expert colleagues appreciatively. Some ministers will not, unfortunately, and it is then your duty to save them from themselves by making sure that the Chief Whip is aware that knowledgeable people are expressing concern. You may just save the government from an abject failure, although the minister concerned may blame you for upsetting his plans and you will have to be content with the knowledge that you have been doing good by stealth.

When trouble strikes, there is no substitute for being out on the ground. When your colleagues are really plotting a big rebellion or are conspiring against the Prime Minister, you will get an idea of what's going on by just walking around the building. Stoll through the ground floor of Portcullis House and see who is having coffee with whom. Sit for a while over your own drink and watch the comings and goings. You will see the alliances forming in your own party or who is in contact with the opposition with your own eyes. On summer nights, sit on the terrace and have a drink with your friends and watch once again who is meeting whom. You can see people whispering in corners when they are plotting and, although you would think that MPs would know better than to plot in full view of the Whips' Office, they still do. You won't know what is being said, of course, but certain combinations of people will be enough to alert you to what is going on. One former minister, currently in the Lords, was an inveterate plotter against the Prime Minister, and her appearance in the tea room was enough to alert any whip in the vicinity to the fact that dirty deeds were afoot. When things were going well, she was hardly ever seen, but at the first whiff of trouble she would rediscover her old friends in the Commons.

Sources in a minister's private office can also be useful. They are usually friends of friends or someone who has worked for an MP in a previous life. One group of ministers who repeatedly plotted against the Prime Minister had a supper club and, when they were meeting, had the engagement put in their diaries. As we had a contact in one of their offices, the whips always knew the dates they were planning to get together and at whose home. Such an inept group of plotters doesn't deserve to succeed and you might well wonder about the capacity for self-deception among people who think that they should be running the country and yet can't even organise a meeting without their opponents knowing about it. Of course, you are one of their opponents because you are one of the Prime Minister's whips and when you find out something like that is going on, you are duty-bound to say something.

When the plot failed, they vented their anger and frustration on any whip who came their way. They had lost their jobs and some were to lose their seats as well. Of course, people like this will be rude to you but, like bodyguards, you take the bullet for your boss and, if you're not prepared to do that, you shouldn't have joined. You are even allowed to laugh in private. After all, they've lost and you have won. If they had won, you would be on the back benches, so you can indulge in a little triumphalism and let them vent their spleen.

Lots of other information will come to you unasked for and when people don't even know that they're giving it. That is why you should not spend too much time in the Whips' Office. Sit in the tea room or the dining room, join in conversations or just listen to your colleagues and you will have a far better idea of what is really going on and how people feel than you would have any other way. Sometimes they will be rude to you and vent their anger about whatever upsets them. It's nothing personal. You just happen to be the one, very lowly, government member who is there. If you have remembered the advice given in earlier chapters, people will open up and tell you things because they will know that, although you will report back, you are not out to get them into trouble. You are simply taking the temperature of the parliamentary party, because part of your job is to avoid a rift opening up between the government and its own MPs. This is usually the best, most accurate information you will get because, rather than relying on rumour or innuendo, you're getting it straight. You may not like what you hear, but it's your job to listen. You are one of the channels of communication; one of the ways in which backbenchers make their feelings known, and you should let them tell you what they want you to hear.

It's for this reason that whips who spend all their time in the office or with other whips are bad at their job. If you do this, you will certainly know what the government thinks, but you won't know what your backbench colleagues think, and so you will be a very bad whip, cocooned in a world in which everyone agrees with ministers and no backbenchers ever argue about their wise decisions. This will make you feel happy and secure until, out of the blue, the government loses a vote and the Prime Minister wants to know why. It may even lead to your speedy return to the back benches. A large part of your job is to listen. Get used to it.

Chapter 10

How to be mean and nasty

ANDREW GWYNNE INSISTS that I tried to kill him. In fact, he told so many people this that a new member once greeted me with the comment, 'Oh, you're the one who nearly killed Andrew.' I can only plead that it wasn't intentional. If he had died it would have been manslaughter by gross negligence rather than deliberate murder. I wasn't actually trying to put him in the mortuary and leave his wife a widow and his children bereft. All I wanted to do was to get him to a House of Commons vote, but if you are a whip, your colleagues will never hear any plea in mitigation. You are a whip and therefore you must have had base motives.

In a sense, they are right. There will be times when you have to ignore your own feelings and forget what other people would do in similar circumstances. You are not 'other people'. You are one of the Prime Minister's whips and if the Prime Minister needs you to win a vote, that is what you must try to do – whatever happens. Normally, when the government has a solid majority, that's not a problem. You can let the sick stay at home or in their hospital beds. People who have urgent business elsewhere can be allowed off to pursue it. In the last two years of the Labour government, we had a notional majority of sixty-seven. It should have provided us with enough of a cushion to operate a sensible system. However, as discontented former ministers increasingly refused to turn up, and some people who had announced their retirement no longer cared, we found that we could not rely on having a majority from day to day. Some people were disconnected from the whole political process. Others, facing the loss of their seats, were scared of their own shadow. If they received half a dozen postcards asking them to vote against a particular Bill, they would do so, thinking it might save their jobs. It didn't, of course. Telling people that your own party is rubbish, which is what, effectively, they were doing, and then asking them to vote for it, is never a good strategy.

Nevertheless, that was the situation we were in when the Prime Minister, in his wisdom, decided that he would introduce a Bill to allow for a referendum on the Alternative Vote. Some Labour MPs love the idea of this – it's their holy grail, the reason they are in politics. Others hate it with a passionate intensity that they usually reserve only for the Liberal Democrats, or UKIP. Since the latter group are in the majority, it was no surprise that the Whips' Office greeted the news with a collective groan. How the hell were we supposed to get them to vote for something they hated?

At first, we were urged to assure people that they were not voting to support the Alternative Vote, but merely to have a referendum on it. Obviously that was never going to work with an idea that inspired such hatred, so we resorted to telling them that it would never get through the Lords. They could therefore vote for it to save the Prime Minister from the humiliation of having one of his initiatives defeated in the Commons, safe in the knowledge that it would never happen. Only after repeated assurances that this was the honest truth ('Trust me, I'm a whip') did our colleagues reluctantly agree to vote for the measure, which was somehow supposed to restore people's trust in politics.

Still, the Whips' Office was uneasy. No one could be sure what would happen on the night and so the Chief Whip decreed that everyone was to be brought back. I put Andrew's case to the Chief, pointing out that he had been very ill and we should let him stay put. Unfortunately, I was overruled and so I had to tell Andrew to get on a train to London for the vote.

I was despatched to collect him at Euston and had a taxi standing by to whisk him, me and his wife, who had travelled with him, to the House of Commons. I was there in plenty of time. Sadly, the train was not. Texts were exchanged, giving me constant updates on where he had got to, which turned out to be nowhere. The train was stuck. Eventually, it started to move, but very slowly. The clock was ticking and I began to fear that both of us would miss the vote. The battery in my phone was getting low. I hung on as long as I could and then sent one last text to tell him I had to go before jumping into the waiting taxi to get back to the House for ten o'clock.

I made it and Andrew arrived at Euston, whereupon he swiftly collapsed. He managed to get himself into a taxi, however, and made it to the House in time to sit in the family room, attended by his long-suffering wife, so that a Tory whip could check he was there and nod him through. At least they didn't actually make him walk through the lobby, which was a good thing because he probably wouldn't have made it. The next day he was in hospital and diagnosed with a pulmonary embolism. The Prime Minister had gone to personally thank him for getting there and the vote was won by a mile. This did not seem to be any consolation to him, though, judging by the texts he sent me from his hospital bed.

Andrew, to his credit, has never held this against me, apart from telling everyone he meets about my homicidal tendencies. It is no use my repeatedly telling everyone that it was not my decision to bring him down for the vote. If you are a whip, you are culpable and no pleas in mitigation are accepted. I fear that when I finally go to the great Whips' Office in the sky and my obituary is read at the PLP, as is the custom, people will hear the words, 'As a whip, she once nearly killed a popular young member of the PLP, Andrew Gwynne. It was no thanks to her that he survived to become a very effective minister.' Those who have never been whips will be shocked to the core. Those who have been will simply wonder, 'Did he make it to the vote?' Being a whip blunts your senses, it really does.

You just have to accept that there are occasions when the job requires you to be heartless, not to care about who you humiliate or the damage you may inflict. Your job is to deliver the votes, remember. If you aren't prepared to do that, then you should get another job. You may be as reasonable as you can most of the time and follow all the precepts I have laid down about treating people fairly, but there will come a point when humiliation is the only way. That's why I once bawled at one MP in front of a bunch of firemen.

There was a lobby organised by firefighters going on and the MP and I had both gone to the central lobby to look for visiting constituents. I had been trying to find her for some time and knew that she was deliberately avoiding me; I wasn't going to pass up the chance of talking to her when I knew she couldn't escape, so I darted across and asked if she would be voting with the government. She wouldn't give a straight answer. She was clearly fed up and didn't think that her problems were being recognised. She moaned about this and that and then, foolishly, added that she had never been invited to No. 10. I saw my chance and bawled, 'You are telling me that you are not voting with the government because you've not been invited to No. 10?!' It was, I think, the only time I actually shouted at someone.

The firemen all looked round. The MP stuttered that it was not just because of that, but I knew that she had lost the moral high ground. I berated her because she was not voting on a principle but just because she hadn't received an invitation. She yelled back. Most of the people there were listening. Eventually, she stalked off, telling me that she had people to see. One of the firemen who had been waiting for me looked at me and said, 'She gave you what for!' 'Yes,' I said, 'but she will vote with the government.' I was right. Kicking over the traces and refusing to obey the whip might gain you kudos in some circles, if people think it's a matter of principle and that you really disagree with the legislation, but I had just told the whole central lobby, including any passing journalist, that she was doing it out of pique. I knew that she would yell at me but I also knew that my tactic was likely to work and that she would end up voting with us. In return, we did get her an invitation to the next No. 10 reception. It doesn't take much to make some people happy. You may find it odd that such things play on the minds of our elected representatives, but everyone likes their ego to be stroked occasionally. There are not many perks in political life, contrary to what many people think, so you should make sure that they are spread around a bit.

Sadly, not everyone will end up forgiving you after you have either humiliated them or led them in to a medical crisis. Ministers usually fall in to this category, as do their private offices. In fact, the private office is usually less forgiving than the minister. They have their plans for keeping their bosses occupied and sending them off on visits around the country and they do not see why these plans should be disrupted over an insignificant matter like keeping the government in power. In fact, they don't usually care about which government is in power at all, or didn't until they found out that the Tories planned to get rid of many of them.

So they will ring and ring and try to get decisions changed and insist that their minister absolutely must go on a certain visit. When all else fails you will just have to get rough with them. I once told a private secretary that, unless a visit was cancelled, his minister would no longer be a minister. I think he believed that I meant he would be sacked, although I really meant that we would no longer be in government. Such behaviour confirms the view of civil servants that whips are not really government ministers, just a bunch of thugs, but it is sometimes necessary to shock them out of their complacency. They live in a world of carefully written memos and committees and second or third opinions on everything. You live in a world where votes have to be delivered that day and you haven't got the time to play nicely, so telling it like it is becomes the only way to go. They won't like you and, no doubt, they will sit around in their offices and complain about your behaviour, but do you really care? You don't have to work with them unless the Prime Minister suddenly decides to make you a minister in that department, in which case having a reputation as a thug just might prevent them trying to put one over on you. It's tough to have to override your own natural courtesy and gentleness but, if you found it that hard, you wouldn't have been put in the Whips' Office in the first place. Save your kindness for small children and old ladies. In your day job, you can often do without it.

Most ministers, unlike their civil servants, do understand the need to come and vote. However, there are exceptions. These are the people who come to Parliament to be ministers rather than MPs. Once they cease to be ministers, they see no point in staying there and leave for well-paid jobs elsewhere. (You know who you are!) Unfortunately, you will have to deal with these people while they are still in the Commons, and they will be the bane of your life. The only consolation is that you can feel free to be as mean and nasty as you wish to them, because the rest of the parliamentary party won't like them either. Of course, the risk is that if they are highly influential, they will ensure that your career comes to an abrupt end. Since that will probably happen anyway, you might as well enjoy yourself in the meantime.

However, sometimes you need the satisfaction of more immediate action, which is when more devious means are called for. Contrary to what people outside the Whips' Office think, there is no 'black book'. Good whips never write such information down, instead keeping it all in their heads. This means that if someone is really giving you trouble, you will need to tap into the collective memory of the office to find out how they can be brought back into line, or punished for making your life difficult. Long-serving colleagues will know who is having trouble in their constituency, or who is in financial trouble, or even whether they have something in their past they wish to keep hidden. This doesn't have to be criminal, by the way – it may simply be something that they wouldn't want others to know. So you might find a Blairite (or 'moderniser' as they are now called) who's a reformed Trot, or a tribune of the people who has hidden his privileged back-ground. If these people are threatening to vote against the government, a reminder that there are things they wouldn't want their constituency party to know, or a hint of the required help in dealing with those who are trying to deselect them, will usually work wonders. Keep these threats for when you really are up against it, though, as you can only use them once. If you threaten someone and fail to carry out your threat, even the dimmest MP will eventually cotton on to the fact that you have no intention of carrying it out. You wouldn't, would you?

Sadly, the House of Commons has reduced some of the whips' powers of patronage by deciding to elect members and chairs of select committees, so telling people that they won't get on the committee they want is now not possible. You can't even threaten that they won't get support from the whips, since whips' support is the kiss of death for anyone who wants to get elected. However, you still have some weapons in your armoury. Office space is, as I mentioned, very limited and some offices do not even have a window. As a consequence, new MPs are desperate to get an office and then even more desperate to get a nice one next time around. Since the whips allocate offices, your power can be used as either a carrot or a stick. One former minister found himself stuck in an office with no windows after he had been particularly critical of the government, and newer MPs can be enticed with the thought of a better office next time there's a move around if you want to keep them on the straight and narrow. Former whips, of course, all have nice offices.

If an MP dies, the first comment is always 'How sad', but the second is 'Where was his office?' On these occasions, however deep your grief, you should realise that you have been presented with a rare opportunity. If your deceased colleague had a decent office, and if someone has been in the House for a while they usually have, then you can keep colleagues in line for weeks by dangling the hope that they might succeed him or her in the place with a window that has now, tragically, been vacated. You should not promise the place to anyone immediately because you will lose the chance of keeping several people slavishly supporting the government for several weeks. You can first say that no decisions will be taken until after the funeral because the family need time to grieve and to arrange for possessions to be collected and for the office to be cleared. This has the great merit of being true and proves that even whips have a heart. Then you can tell them that no decisions will be made until after the by-election, when you will know whether you have to accommodate a new colleague or to arrange a general move around to fit in a member of the opposition. No accommodation whip worth his salt will ever give one of the better offices to a new member. If that happened, what would they have to aspire to in the future? Whips are caring souls.

Another weapon in your armoury is the way in which people are allocated to Bill committees. If you really want to punish someone, you can make them a member of the longest, most boring Committee Stage you can find, dealing with a subject in which they have absolutely no interest.

It will use up their time on Tuesdays and Thursdays for weeks on end, while giving them no political advantage whatsoever. Still, you need to be careful. Really difficult types will retaliate either by not turning up when you need them, or by making long, boring speeches that delay the business and drive your colleagues insane.

You can also do the opposite and refuse to put people on a committee in which they have a real interest. Someone with real expertise in a subject might long to do a particular Bill. Strange, I know, but politicians are strange people and some of them do have a genuine interest in odd subjects. Ensuring that the whip in charge of the Bill refuses to put them on a committee, however good a speech they have made in the Second Reading debate, will drive them nuts. You can then explain that you are doing this because you feel that they are not helpful to the government. They will usually deny it and promise you their absolute loyalty, in which case you can see if they are prepared to demonstrate it by putting them on another Bill committee that they definitely *don't* want to be on (see above). You can do this, comfortable in the knowledge that you are doing a favour for the minister who is taking the Bill through. Experts are dangerous. They may know more than the minister and, when they criticise the Bill, they may well be right. You do not want them proving that in public.

Trips can be another source of harmless fun with people who give you grief. There are always delegations to other countries and select committee trips being arranged, although some MPs are now reluctant to go overseas for fear of being accused of junketing. There will be times when you need to refuse to allow people to go for very good reasons, such as the government being in danger of losing a vote. Indeed, in bad times, people have been stopped at the airport and told to turn back, and ministers have landed after a long trip only to be told to get back on the plane and come home again.

When you are not under pressure, trips are a valuable tool for punishment and reward. A quiet word by your Chief or Deputy to the Commonwealth Parliamentary Association of the Inter-Parliamentary Union that a certain person might cause embarrassment is usually enough to ensure that they aren't selected for a particular visit. If you really want to be difficult, you can let someone be selected and then refuse to pair them. All these visits rely on agreements between whips to make sure that the government keeps in majority. When things are tight, it means that only if an equal number of government and opposition MPs are away can the trip proceed. When the government has a bigger majority, the numbers are adjusted accordingly and there will be more government than opposition MPs, keeping the balance in the House. Still, a good whip can always foresee an imminent rebellion, which means that some people will not be allowed to go. You can get the Deputy to decide that only equal numbers can go, even if you have a large majority, because a storm is coming. This can never be disproved because, in politics, there is always a storm coming, it's just that you don't know when. Sadly, therefore, one or more people will be unable to join this valuable delegation and will have to wait for another opportunity.

One word of warning, though. If you are going to pull stunts like this, make sure that they are only used if people have been really difficult for a long time. They should never be used on people who have a genuine issue of conscience to struggle with, as you will only alienate them for ever. Save these strategies for those who vote against the government repeatedly or who constantly fail to turn up for votes. Then you have a justification for being mean and nasty. After all, they deserve it.

Chapter 11

How to socialise

YOU'RE A HARD-WORKING whip and may think that you have no time for fripperies. The government is depending on you to get its legislation through and to stop things falling apart, or so you think. Well, think again. Firstly, you are only a small cog helping to turn the great wheel of government. Secondly, socialising is now part of your job. You don't have to enjoy it – in fact, you probably won't most of the time – but you must do it, because it's the only way of finding out what your colleagues really think about the issues facing the government. You need to spend time talking with them and, more importantly, listening to them, and you will not get far with this unless they trust you.

There are whips who are more hard-line and more paranoid than senior ministers looking over their shoulders at rivals. They report back every disagreement with government policy, however minor, even if the person concerned has no intention of voting against the government. They see every deviation from the official line, however stupid that line may be, as a sign of imminent social breakdown and the precursor of political annihilation, which must therefore be stamped out. I had a whip like this when I first entered Parliament. As I was naturally a gobby sod who, in the great northern female tradition, was not slow to voice my opinions, I was soon on the whip's list of untrustworthy people, even though I consistently voted with the government. The result was that I hardly talked to her and didn't give her my view on anything. When I finally did decide to vote against something, there was no chance of persuading me otherwise (and I thought the policy was terrible anyway!).

This is really bad whipping and you should never do it. Let people have their grumble. They will feel better for it and you should be grown up enough to understand that all political parties are coalitions. No one is ever going to agree 100 per cent with everything in the manifesto or be wildly enthusiastic about everything their own government does. If they do, they're too stupid to ever be a minister and, if they rise to that position, as people like this invariably want to, you should view them as a disaster waiting to happen because people who never question anything are suckers for whatever daft policy the civil service puts in front of them.

So, keep in touch with the rest of your colleagues. The tea room, the dining room and, occasionally, the bar are part of your workplace even more than the Whips' Office is. Only whips inhabit the office and you can assume they're going to support the government, so get out and talk to other people. By 'talk', I mean take part in normal conversations. Sit there with your tea or coffee and go with the flow. You will learn far more about what is on people's minds than you will ever find out through one of the 'ring-rounds' that whips are required to undertake from time to time. Indeed, if you don't gain people's trust by sitting and talking to them and not reporting every tiny piece of dissent on to those above you, you will have little chance of getting the truth out of them when it really matters.

You may think that when you are sitting around like this, people will think that you are not working. They will. Let them do so, because you know better. A good Chief or Deputy Chief Whip will not only know what you are doing on such occasions, but will expect you to spend part of your day doing it. So do it and expect that your colleagues, supportive as ever, will pull your leg and wonder why you haven't got any work to do. They will, in the pleasant banter common to all in the parliamentary party, suggest that you are being paid for doing nothing, wonder who's keeping the government on the road and suggest that you come back to the back benches where all the real hard work is done. Sit and take it. At least it's a conversation opener.

You should diary in some time every day when you will be in the tea room or one of the other venues where MPs congregate for breaks or meals. Make sure that you don't stick to the same place all the time. MPs are creatures of habit and all have their favourite places on the parliamentary estate. Go to the tea room one day, the downstairs cafeteria the next, Portcullis House at another time. Every so often, simply have a walk around the place and see who you encounter. The library, the lady Members' rooms and the terrace are all places where you can pass the time of day with your colleagues and join in their conversations.

In the evenings, you should eat in the dining room whenever you can. Sometimes this will be difficult because the bench rota or the business of the House means that you will be eating at odd times, but when you can get in there, you must. Sit wherever there is a space instead of looking for a table where your particular friends are eating and you might find that different company proves entertaining. Whatever happens, you should never, ever sit down with a table full of whips. You can talk to them at any time and all your party colleagues will simply assume that you are plotting some nefarious deed even if you are all talking about the football. In any case, plotting is serious stuff, which should only be done in the Whips' Office. Sitting at a table where one other whip is present or allowing one other to join you is permissible as long as there are plenty of non-whips around too.

Likewise, you should not join a table full of ministers. Many of them have a regrettable tendency to congregate together, either because they believe they have important issues to discuss or because they want to keep an eye on one another.

This prevents them talking to backbenchers and makes them very unpopular. While you need not worry about them, you should be worried about what the backbenchers think because you want happy backbenchers who will support the government, not MPs who think they are not listened to and are of no account. This problem was pointed out to ministers several times when I was a whip, but some of them still did not get it and were then genuinely surprised when their legislation ran into trouble and no one was inclined to listen to their attempts to explain it.

'Can I ever eat with my friends?' you may ask plaintively. The answer is yes, occasionally. After all, you will want them to still be your friends when you are sacked or leave office. Just explain to them that you can't do it as often as you used to and that it is not helpful if they wave across the dining room when you are sitting with other people and shout, 'Oh, you're being a whip tonight, are you?' That really puts a stop to any decent conversations, believe me. If all else fails, you can threaten that no one will get a lift home or share your car to the station on a Thursday night ever again if they try to be funny. Bribery usually works when an appeal to their better natures might fail.

Even if you are not a drinker, you will need to appear in the bar from time to time. The reason is simple. You can find people down in the bar who you can never find anywhere else. Especially when the House is sitting late, many people will go there for some company and, of course, for the drink. They are generally a happy group, especially after a few pints, so it's not hard to be nice to them. The one golden rule is that you must not get drunk. Life is unfair and people have the general view that whips running the business ought to stay sober, especially female whips (I said it was unfair). Besides, a whip is never really off-duty and, if you move up the hierarchy in the Whips' Office, you could be called on to deal with a sudden crisis. It's no use thinking that you can foresee when these will happen. If they were foreseeable then there wouldn't be a crisis, so keep to the golden rule and stay sober. Buy your round early and then nurse your drink carefully as you wander from group to group. A cheerful 'I've got one, thanks' will mean you can avoid another drink. If you are really pressed, saying that you are on duty later will do. MPs, generally, know that it's unwise to appear in the chamber the worse for wear, particularly if you are a whip. Besides, if you are going to socialise with your colleagues on a regular basis, you need to find a way of doing it without ruining your health. Fortunately, there is much less of a drinking culture in the House than there was years ago, which will make your job much easier.

Drinking less will also ensure that you are more likely to keep your job. All whips, especially the more senior ones, work long hours. 'First in and last out' is the rule, and you will find that appearing frequently with a hangover does your career prospects no good at all. You will spend your time dealing with confidential issues and nobody trusts a drunk.

The one time you should never socialise on the premises is when you have delivered the government a victory in a controversial vote. You will certainly feel like doing so. Being a whip is stressful and there will be times when everyone wants to let off steam. After all, you have undergone days, maybe even weeks, of working non-stop. You have toiled hard to deliver a vote against all the odds and you will feel that your triumphs should be celebrated or your hard work rewarded. You have cajoled, persuaded and even bullied people into voting with the government. You have tracked down the missing, maybe even turning them around at the airport or bringing them back from trips abroad. You have brought in the sick who should have been left at home and all this has resulted in a government victory, which the press were probably saying was impossible only a few days ago.

You, understandably, want to celebrate this remarkable feat. Don't. If you have just delivered a vote for the Prime Minister that no one thought you could win, remember that there will be a lot of people feeling very bruised. Those in your own party who voted against you will be feeling sick, especially if they thought they had a good cause. Others may have voted against for good reasons and watched in despair as they saw the vote lost. The people you persuaded will still be wondering if they have done the right thing, and those who were bullied or threatened will be feeling sore. Some you will have dragooned through the lobby against their better judgement and some will have voted purely out of loyalty while feeling in their bones that the government has got it wrong. Whips never admit this, of course, but it is sometimes true. The last thing either of these two groups of people will wish to see is a group of whips partying. First, it will seem as if you are celebrating conning them into doing something they felt was wrong. Second, it will look as if you are rubbing their noses in it. You will have to build bridges with all these people if you want to continue to work with them, so consider their feelings.

As for the people you stopped from going on trips or brought back from abroad, they will hate the sight of you. The sick you brought back are usually remarkably forgiving since you will, of course, have only brought in people guaranteed to support the government, but they are still unwell and need cherishing. Devote your time to making sure they are escorted back home and made comfortable rather than anything else and they will thank you for it.

If you want to celebrate, do it off the premises and in reasonable privacy. Even those who voted with you do not enjoy the sight of triumphant whips laughing over their dinner and ordering bottles of wine. Such behaviour will merely confirm the whips' reputation for being a callous bunch of unfeeling bastards. While this may be true, it's not the impression you want to cultivate. The wounds that accompany such a split will heal much more quickly if you avoid any hint of triumphalism, and a happy and reasonably united party in the future will make your job so much easier.

It may be that, after a crucial vote, you will be invited to a Downing Street reception. Prime Ministers have been known to do this if there is something going on that evening. If so, it's usual to take advantage of the offer since the drink will be free and the Prime Minister will feel snubbed if you don't go. (A hint – he is your boss.) However, while getting your hands on as much free wine as you can, you are still expected to behave with some decorum. Even the Whips' Office has some standards and the other people there are the PM's guests. Try to remember that.

Chapter 12

How to ignore
the big stuff

YOU ARE A member of the government. All around
you, people are drafting policies, deciding how to
deal with the great issues of the day (or, at least, letting other people tell them how to deal with them).
You sit in on their meetings so you will know something about
what is being planned. You may even know things they don't
want you to know because it's your job to find them out. You
feel right in the centre of things.

The problem is that you do not make the decisions. You
are there to implement other people's decisions, whether

you like them or not. Most of the time you will find this immensely frustrating, particularly when you feel something is going wrong in an area of policy that you know a lot about.

This doesn't mean that you need to leave your brain down in reception when you head off to your department for a ministerial meeting. Your job is to spot the flaws in a minister's plans, but the problems you are looking for relate to whether you can get the policy voted through the Commons. You may believe it's a good policy but one many MPs will not like, in which case you should tell the ministers concerned and help them find a way of dealing with their objections. Or it may be so misconceived and dangerous for the government that you should alert the Chief Whip immediately, especially when you believe a minister is trying to undermine the Prime Minister. At times like this, you hope that the Chief Whip will be able to use his authority to put a stop to whatever crazy scheme is being drawn up without delay. It will be dealt with way above your pay grade and you should be thankful for that.

You are allowed to be interested in policy; after all, you are still a politician, and what is decided will impact on the people you represent, but you should try to see this as a hobby you pursue in private. Your day-to-day concerns will be very different, and you have to be able not to sweat the big stuff and hope that someone else is dealing with it. When they don't, you will be around to pick up the pieces. That's a whip's job.

To give an example, when the banks began to collapse, chaos reigned in Whitehall. We were being called into regular meetings to be told what the government was doing.

My colleagues who bore the ancient title of Lords Commissioners of Her Majesty's Treasury found themselves being called in at short notice, often in the middle of the night. On one particular night, just as the collapse was beginning, one of them was summoned to the Treasury at two in the morning. He was, naturally, not best pleased. He walked in, cursing the idiot civil servants who could not get things done during the day, then saw what was happening. The place was full of people, rushing around. A very senior civil servant, known for his immaculate dress and unflappability, a stereotypical Whitehall mandarin, was coming down the stairs, his hair askew and looking as if he hadn't slept for several nights. He wore no jacket and his shirt was covered in huge patches of sweat.

The whip took one look at him and decided it was probably best not to complain about being woken up in the middle of the night. He signed the documents he was given and was then locked in a room until the markets opened, so sensitive were they.

Similar incidents took place with worrying regularity as the government attempted to get to grips with the crisis until, finally, one of the Lords Commissioners revolted. He would put up with being woken in the middle of the night, signing documents to make sure that a financial system did not collapse. He accepted that he would have to be tucked away until the markets opened because the information was so market-sensitive. What he could not accept, however, was that the entire Treasury staff could not find him a cup of tea or a bacon sandwich during all the time he was locked away. He refused to come again unless they gave him some breakfast. They did.

On another day, someone walked into the office and announced, 'I've just bought a bank!' He had signed the papers to bring it into public ownership. He insisted on having a copy to show his grandchildren.

Yet, although they are needed to carry out some of the basic tasks, in such a crisis, whips are not at the heart of the process because they are not taking the decisions. Their job is not to worry about the decision-making (although it is hard not to when the world economic system is collapsing around you), but to reassure everyone else, to keep the show on the road and to make sure that the business is dealt with as usual, or as usual as it can be when the Chancellor and the Prime Minister have to keep coming to Parliament to make emergency statements. The only way to cope with it is to develop a grim sense of humour and to hope others are doing their job while you are doing yours. Granted that this is difficult, given the general Whips' Office view about ministers, but it has to be done.

So blasé did we become that documents to seize Icelandic assets in Britain were signed over a whips' breakfast one morning. Civil servants came in quietly while we were waiting for the meeting to start and signatures were scrawled.

'What are you doing?' someone enquired.

'Seizing Icelandic assets under the Prevention of Terrorism Act,' came the laconic response.

Everyone started paying attention suddenly.

'Are the Icelanders terrorists?' said a voice stifled by a mouthful of bacon butty.

We all paused to think.

'Well,' came the response, 'they did fight the Cod War.'

Then we carried on.

If it was the only way to save something for those who had lost money in Icelandic banks, then we were not going to quarrel with it. One day, when those documents are released from the archives, people will wonder why they have grease stains on them.

As the meltdown in the financial markets coincided with my entrance to the Whips' Office, I lived with it for most of my time there, yet it impacted very little on my day-to-day work (apart from minor details like leading into a disastrous general election). On the Wednesday after I was appointed, Spads from No. 10 and the Treasury joined us at breakfast to explain the situation. Northern Rock had been taken into public owner-ship earlier that year but the turmoil in the markets was now getting worse. The government had already had to intervene to prevent Bradford & Bingley going under and was now inject-ing more money into the system, recapitalising the banks and taking preference shares, as well as underwriting bank debts in an attempt to get lending started again.

Yet, we walked back to the House in a cheerful mood. A crisis is helpful to whips. No one wants to be seen indulging in petty rebellions or undermining their own government at a time of great national crisis (well, not many of them any-way). So one whip sat at his desk singing the *Bob the Builder* theme ('Can he fix it? Yes he can!') and Alistair Darling got a good reception as he came to make yet another statement.

And what was my task for the day? It was to make sure that a statutory instrument got through a committee at 4.30 that afternoon. Since no one really wants to do these committees because they are likely to induce death from terminal boredom, two people had dropped out at the last minute for fairly spurious reasons. I spent my time, therefore, not worrying about the financial crisis, but begging, pleading, cajoling and calling in favours until I found two people who could replace them. When I got there, I found that the room was full of Tories. I hastily counted the members of the committee and found that we hadn't got a majority. Only a week into the job, and I was going to have to go back and report my abject failure to the Deputy Chief Whip. Jumping out of the window into the Thames seemed preferable.

I counted and counted again, desperate for my figures to be wrong, but it was no good. We still didn't have a majority. I checked with the clerks that the Tories who weren't on the committee could not vote. Even though I knew this was the case, I needed to hear someone say it. Perhaps, I thought hopefully, this was one of the tricks people played on new whips, but, no, they all looked far too serious for that. With seconds to go, the last people came in and we had a majority. I had lost years off my life and could have cheerfully killed them, but they came in as if they hadn't a care in the world. As far as they were concerned, they had got there on time, so there was no problem. Nothing could illustrate better the difference between the way a whip sees the world and the way it is perceived by everyone else. The Tories talked for a long time but it didn't matter: we had the votes. I heaved a sigh of relief. The strange thing is that I cannot remember now what the committee was about. My job was to win the vote and I did. Process had taken over from substance, just as it does for most whips, most of the time anyway.

The same strange disjuncture between what was going on inside Parliament and what was happening outside could be seen in the chamber as the evening wore on. We were dealing with the Children's Bill and MPs who had long wanted to ban the physical punishment of children had tabled an amendment that would do this. They saw it as a reasonable measure, building on the ban on corporal punishment in schools. I agreed with them but, unfortunately, the government did not. Ministers were terrified of being accused of interfering in people's homes and incurring the wrath of the *Daily Mail*. They are always frightened of the *Mail*. If we got to a vote, the result was likely to be a split in the party, with many usually loyal people going into the lobby to oppose their own government.

The Chief Whip had decided this was the last thing we needed in the current climate, so he introduced an ordering motion to change the sequence in which amendments were debated. Physical punishment would come last. This was the occasion when he offered a bottle of champagne to anyone who could speak, and call a vote on, the Ten Minute Rule motion that preceded the main business. It was one of those rare occasions when we abandoned our usual practice of not voting on these Bills, lingering in the lobby for as long as possible and encouraging all our colleagues to have long conversations with any minister they had been trying to nab for weeks.

Ministers were instructed to give really detailed answers to any points their colleagues raised on the Bill and did so, proving there is a first time for everything. Our people duly cooperated by making long speeches and intervening as often as possible. Indeed, they were so cooperative that I began to suspect that many of them did not want to reach the crucial vote any more than we did. They might support a ban in principle, but they did not wish to incur the wrath of the right-wing tabloids. They had enough troubles already. I watched Greg Pope, who had moved the amendment, shrug his shoulders resignedly. He was a former whip and he knew an operation when he saw one.

We never reached the amendment and experienced the satisfaction of a job well done. That, together with winning the vote in committee, meant that I went home tired but happy, and I could see the same expression on the faces of other whips. We had been at work since breakfast and had been on our feet all day, organising speakers and making sure all went according to plan. Our job had been done. We ended the day with a united party, no big rows and the government's business successfully through the Commons. The rest was for others to worry about. We went home smiling and feeling as if we had a grip on things. Outside, the financial markets were still in meltdown.

If you cannot cope with such a gap between experience in the Commons and the reality outside, then you should not ever accept a job in the Whips' Office. The job description requires you to blank out many of the important things that are happening and concentrate on the moment. Whips want simple things: a happy and united party, an easy progress for government legislation and no cock-ups on the floor of the House or in committee. Since the world does not run like this, they are constantly disappointed and continually fighting to achieve those ends. So their universe narrows down to what they have to deliver, what is to be done that day. It is not that you should be unaware of what is going on elsewhere, but that you have to leave it to others to deliver the solutions; admittedly a difficult task when you think of some of the ministers involved. Focusing on the narrow canvass that you deal with is essential to avoid a mental meltdown.

We were to find that, as the government staggered on to electoral defeat, we were constantly firefighting. Most mornings we would come in to work and someone would say cheerily, 'And today's crisis is?' The key to surviving in these circumstances is to solely concentrate on what you have to do that day, to maintain a close relationship with the other people in the office and to celebrate your triumphs when they happen. The Whips' Office is definitely a team operation: a win for one is a win for all and an injury to one is an injury to all. You will learn that a defeat for the government is seen as a personal failure, while a win runs through your veins like a glass of champagne, but you must never start measuring the size of a defeat against the size of a victory. Take each day as it comes, for you will have enough to worry about within that twenty-four hours without bothering about anything else.

Sometimes this will be exceptionally difficult. At one point, when the government was lurching from one crisis to another and the media were whipping up a fury at MPs' expenses, I spent my time looking for a hat.

Abusive emails were coming in day by day accusing me of numerous crimes and misdemeanours, none of which I had actually committed. One came from someone we traced to a website on which he applauded the killing of the Swedish foreign minister. Youngsters going home from the pub would regularly stop outside the house at 1 a.m. and shout abuse. I was getting off lightly compared to some MPs. Most were living on their nerves; their children were being bullied at school, their husbands and wives abused in the street. People were suffering panic attacks.

Yet, I had to attend the royal garden parties, as is the duty of those whips who hold titles in the royal household. My two colleagues could wear the morning dress they had had to buy for the State Opening of Parliament. I had to explain that I could not wear the same outfit three times. I had one dress that was suitable and I spent my free time desperately looking for another outfit that fitted the palace rules. The Deputy Chief Whip was also insisting that I wore a hat. I hardly ever wear hats and those I did possess were designed to keep me warm when I was canvassing in winter. So I dutifully traipsed from shop to shop one weekend, desperate to find something. I even got a text from the civil servants in our back office saying that the Deputy had asked them to remind me to get a hat.

Eventually, I found one. I was worn out, almost buckling under the pressure we faced, and I'd wasted most of my weekend. Yet, I would not let the side down. I would be suitably dressed to walk up and down a Buckingham Palace lawn, where no one would really care who I was or what I was wearing at all. At the time, banks were collapsing, the entire financial system was on the verge of collapse and most government ministers were desperately trying to save the economy and prevent the government from going under with it. Not me. I was looking for a hat because I couldn't go to see the Queen without one. If there is anything that better demonstrates the absurdity of how we run our politics, I have yet to come across it. You too will no doubt think that this demonstrates a skewed sense of priorities. If you want to say so, I wish you well, but you will need an understanding Deputy Chief Whip.

Of course, this is ludicrous and the custom should be abolished. In such circumstances you will have better things to do, even if there is not a major crisis building up; but if you sign on for the Whips' Office, you sign on for everything that goes with it, good and bad. We all went off to the garden party in our best finery, even though things were getting so bad that we expected that one day we might find one of our colleagues dead. We smiled and did what we had to do nonetheless. We were whips.

The difficulty of shutting yourself off and concentrating on your own job becomes progressively more difficult when you know the truth about some cock-up or that plans are afoot that will really annoy your own backbenchers. If you are going to be a whip, you will find yourself in that position frequently. You know that the government is planning a course of action that will enrage the members of your party, you will have discussed it in the whips' meeting and you will be well aware sometimes that the Chief, knowing full well what the consequences will be, is trying to get it stopped. Unfortunately, when your colleagues get wind of what is going on, you will not be able to tell them that you too think it is the maddest idea you have ever heard and that only a minister on magic mushrooms could have come up with it. Instead, your job is to smile and tell them not to worry. If they persist (and they will, for they are politicians too) you are permitted to smile knowingly and tell them that it is all being taken care of, while fervently hoping that what you are saying is true. This was the case when Jack Straw announced that he had made a commitment to raise the pay of the Parliamentary Commissioner for Standards and the Head of the Electoral Commission. I went round the tea room assuring MPs fizzing with anger that, yes, we knew how they felt, and that, don't worry, it was all being taken care of. Well, at least we were trying.

Even worse was the occasion when the newspapers revealed a leaked plan that said the government had planned to raise VAT to 18.5 per cent. The papers were full of 'Labour's Tax Bombshell' stories and it was clear that the posting of the document on the Treasury website was part of a deliberate campaign of leaks against the government. Presumably the civil servants involved in these leaks were desperate to see a government that sacked a lot of their colleagues, privatised many of the services they provided and held down their wages. There's nowt so queer as folk.

As Labour MPs, who were already unhappy, grew more and more jittery about their chances of holding onto their seats, Treasury Spads were despatched to brief the whips. It did not go well. After assuring us that the document concerned was only one of several options under discussion, they then went on to say that, even if we had raised VAT (which wasn't going to happen, of course), then people on lower incomes would not be worse off. The scepticism that greeted this assurance must have been obvious even to them.

It increased immediately when they went on to tell us that, if VAT was raised (which, of course, wasn't going to happen), then the rise in personal allowances, which had been introduced following the abolition of the 10p tax rate, would more than compensate lower earners. The whips around the table put on their 'Do you really think we're stupid enough to believe that?' faces but apparently the Spads, used to the rarefied and academic atmosphere of the Treasury, did. The mutterings and growls of discontent from those who lived in the world of constituency surgeries and door-knocking increased. We didn't like it. What was more, we knew the PLP would like it even less. People already had their money from the rise in personal allowances. They'd budgeted for it and were using it and would be as likely to see it as compensating for a future VAT rise as any of us was to become Chancellor of the Exchequer. Come to think of it, if any of us did, it might not be a bad idea considering the rubbish that was now being floated.

The Spads went on their way to kick around more daft policy ideas and we left and went grumbling all the way back to the Commons. Such mad ideas did not seem to have any connection with the real world in which we lived.

But did we voice any of these concerns outside the office? Of course we didn't. We did our job, which was to assure our colleagues that everything was being dealt with, it was a stupid idea floated by a civil servant and there was no way it was going to happen. Whether that was true or not, we didn't know. Whether any of our colleagues believed us was even more doubtful, but it was our job to sound as if we believed it, to calm the troops, to reassure and to make sure that business proceeded as normal, so that is what we did. All the while, we were hoping that someone, somewhere, well above our pay grade, was working to make sure that the idea was killed off. It was the kind of blind leap of faith that whips have to take every day, or at least con themselves into believing they are taking. Switch off the worries and attend to the business – it's what being a whip requires. Then you can go home and, in the privacy of your own flat, with no colleagues to talk to and no family around to distract you, you can worry as much as you like. No one will know and you can give yourself up to your worst imaginings. The next morning, you can go straight back to portraying an attitude of absolute faith in government ministers who will never land their colleagues in trouble and never take action that will lose people their seats. If you can fake this, you'll be a good whip. As long, of course, as you know you're faking it.

Chapter 13

How to deal with a crisis

THE FIRST RULE for dealing with a crisis caused by a whip is to understand that they never happen. Just as when the government does something stupid, it is essential that your demeanour always conveys that everything is going according to plan. When the business is in a mess, when votes have been lost, when the opposition are keeping your colleagues up all night and they're getting more and more fractious every hour, you should always look as if this is just what you expected and everything is going swimmingly. It is harder to maintain this illusion with those who have been whips themselves and who will know what is going wrong, but you should try it with most of your colleagues.

When there is a personal scandal involving one or more of your MPs, when a minister has made an outrageous gaffe or when the papers are filled with headlines about fallings-out within the government, even a whip cannot hope to pretend that these events were planned, since, if you are out to cause trouble for the government, you should not be a whip. On these occasions, you should adopt the pretence of knowing far more than you do and assure everyone that the problem is being dealt with. It probably is being dealt with, somewhere, although the outcome is usually not what you would hope.

The real dividing line is between a crisis that stays within the Whips' Office and one that happens outside. Problems may be caused when one of your own whips makes a mistake and you may be cursing and swearing inside the office, but you will never, ever blame them to anyone else. Whips look after their own, however catastrophic the mistake might have been, and if anyone else does notice (and sometimes it is so bad that they can't help but pick it up), then you should make light of it. Tell everyone it's just a minor error that can easily be put right. It usually can and whips should avoid showing panic at all costs.

One whip once lost a vote in committee because he had forgotten what Labour policy was. When an amendment was put to the vote, he shouted 'aye' and the other members of the committee, who were probably spending their time doing their post or writing future speeches, obediently followed him. The excuse that he gave to the Chief Whip for voting against Labour policy, and getting others to vote with him, was that what was in the amendment had been Labour policy, but the policy had just changed. The truth was that he had been discussing who was the prettiest of the Hansard shorthand writers, with a minister, during a particularly boring part of the proceedings and had been distracted. The Chief shouted and swore at him in the privacy of his office and told him, with a fair sprinkling of expletives, to 'put it right'. It was done by overturning the committee vote when the Bill returned to the floor of the House, but not a word was said outside.

Another, unfortunately, had no idea of what she was doing. Not only was she letting too many people miss committee and therefore failing to maintain a government majority, but she was also spending time tweeting rather than watching what was going on. As a result, she had been failing to get people back from outside the committee room for votes. The full story was brought to me by a friend of mine who served on the Chairmen's Panel, the group of MPs who preside over committees, and who was unlucky enough to be chairing this particular fiasco.

'I tried to indicate to her that she needed to get people back before we locked the doors,' said my friend unhappily, 'but she didn't seem to pick up on it.' What made matters worse was that one vote had been lost first thing in the morning. Not everyone had arrived, but the minister had said only a few words in reply to a debate, which had begun in the previous session, and then sat down. He had not had the sense to keep talking until everyone arrived and the whip had not had the sense to tell him to do so. The Tories, scenting blood, had all arrived bang on time and we lost yet another vote.

I sighed and went to see the Deputy Chief Whip, who already had part of the story. He shook his head as we discussed it and commented that the person concerned was a nice woman who should never have been made a whip. Then he spent a lot of time sitting in the committee making sure that such a disaster did not happen again. The votes we had lost were reversed on the floor of the House later but, and this is the significant thing, the problem was never mentioned outside the Whips' Office. Only a few people on the committee realised what had happened and the reputation of this particular MP remained intact, although it was, in our view, overinflated. Another role was found for her eventually, which took her away from running government business. The office never does down its own, even when everyone knows that a particular person has been an idiot, or worse than an idiot. Mistakes are dealt with. Deliberate wrongdoing will get you gently pushed aside.

Leaking to the press is the worst offence that you can commit, but even that will be dealt with 'in-house'. Whips should never give interviews and should avoid lunches or dinners with journalists. You know too much and a few glasses of wine can always lead people into saying more than they mean to. Just remember that you are called 'the silent whip' in the House of Commons for a good reason – you are meant to keep what you know under your hat, even if that hat is bought only for a garden party.

Only once did I know a whip to leak. A story appeared in one of the papers about tension between the Chief Whip and another Cabinet minister, suggesting that the Chief was trying to scupper his legislation. Naturally, he was furious. Chief Whips who appear in the papers are not doing their job properly. The essence of a good Chief Whip is absolute discretion and ours was famous for it. He was the kind of man who wouldn't even confirm today's date to a journalist without giving it serious thought. On that occasion, he felt that the story made him look bad and assumed it had been leaked by another minister.

Unfortunately, I knew that his assumption wasn't true. I knew which whip had been having lunch with the journalist involved the day before the story had appeared, because I had been in the office when she set off and she had made no secret of where she was going. If you find yourself in these circumstances, you may well be reluctant to drop a colleague right in it. Sorry, but you gave up the right to those feelings of human sympathy when you joined. Your loyalty is to the Chief Whip and to the Prime Minister who appointed you. Your job is to see that government business runs smoothly and it will not run smoothly if two Cabinet ministers suspect one another of leaking. In a situation like this, there is only one thing to be done. Tell the Deputy what you know or think you know. Tell him quietly out of the hearing of others and then leave him to get on with it. Don't run a vendetta against the leaker by telling everyone else in your office, even though you will certainly feel like doing so. Leaking may be the worst crime a whip can commit, but leaking against one of your own is definitely an aggravating factor that calls for an exemplary sentence. Let it happen, but let it be dealt with way above your pay grade. In this case, it was, and there were no more leaks. Nor did anyone outside the Whips' Office ever get to know what happened. You don't only look after your own, but you never, ever wash your dirty linen in public.

A crisis which is not of your making is not so easy to keep quiet. In fact, the first you will hear of it is likely to be when you open the papers on Sunday morning. For this reason, you should make sure you get a couple of the tabloids delivered even if you only scan them to make sure that none of your flock is featured that week. MPs are remarkably Micawberish when they are in trouble. They persist in believing that something will turn up to help them and that the worst will not happen right up until the presses are rolling, the early editions hit the streets and other journalists have started to camp outside their homes. The last people they tell are the whips, believing that you will use their indiscretions against them and, let's face it, in a crunch you probably would. They will then call on you for help when the shit hits the fan and expect you to save them and their seats.

The first thing you need to ask is the simple whip's question: 'Sex or money?' Sexual misconduct can probably be dealt with. It will be awful for the person involved, and even worse for his wife or family, but the damage often fades with time. Financial dishonesty is a whole different ball game and can (and should) be career-ending. You may ask why I assume that anyone involved in sexual misconduct will be male. It's not sexism so much as knowledge of life in the House of

Commons. Elegant and beautiful young women, whether they be researchers, journalists looking for a story or hangers-on, often gravitate to middle-aged, male MPs, presumably attracted by the idea of power (before they discover their target hasn't got any) and their male target is so flattered he doesn't bother to ask why a pretty young woman is interested in a paunchy, balding man. Clue – it is not for his views on the latest statutory instrument committee. It doesn't really work the other way around. Handsome young men do not throw themselves at menopausal women MPs. Firstly, because they are likely to be laughed at and, secondly, because most women would smell a rat immediately. You are far more likely to have to deal with a man who has got himself into that kind of trouble.

Whatever the problem is, you must insist that they tell you the whole story if they want help. If you suspect that they are hiding something, tell them straight out that you can't help them unless they give you the whole truth. If you have to deal with a problem like this, the chances are you will be a senior whip, so use your status and your muscle a bit if they won't open up. Anyone involved has to tell you honestly whether they have done what they are being accused of, or not. Either way, they are likely to need legal advice and the party will know a number of good lawyers it can recommend if they haven't found one already. Next, make sure that their family is being looked after. They are unlikely to be used to being in the public eye and, even for those who are, a pack of journalists on the hunt is not pleasant. Have they got some support or can you arrange for some, perhaps from one of the party's press officers? It may be, of course, that the miscreant's wife is not speaking to him, and you may well feel she's got just cause. However, she might speak to you or to someone else in the Whips' Office if there is anyone there who knows her well. If not, track down the people who do know her and get them to get in touch. The first duty you owe is to the innocent victims of the scandal and this is one occasion where the demands of common humanity coincide exactly with the needs of your party. You absolutely do not want a wronged wife out on the doorstep telling the assembled press corps what a right bastard her husband has been, even if you think he deserves it. Nor do you want one of your MPs arranging one of those cheesy photo shoots with his wife and family to show how they are 'standing by him'. If she has any sense, she is probably standing by him with a large kitchen knife. Anyway, look what a photo like that did for David Mellor.

If possible, you don't want any of the parties talking to the press at all. You need to persuade your MP that 'telling his side of the story' will only make things worse and get him to agree a statement with the party's press officers before shutting up completely. A story can only be kept going if people keep commenting on it. If they keep quiet, then the press has nothing else to print.

Think carefully about exactly what you are dealing with and talk it through with the MP involved. If the story is completely untrue, they are likely to be involved in a future libel action with the terrible prospect of losing and being left with all the costs, since it is possible to lose even if you have done nothing wrong. Like most people, they will find this prospect terrifying and will need your sympathy and support, as well as the support of their colleagues. It is also possible that they have done something really stupid but have been set up by someone acting for the press or someone who has sold their story afterwards. It has happened to several MPs because they were daft enough to believe that the tall, leggy beauty they met in the bar was really, really interested in them and they ignored one of the clear rules of politics, which is never to sleep with anyone who has less to lose than you do. In that case, they have been stupid rather than evil and will also deserve some sympathy, although not as much as the MPs who dutifully go home and ring their wives each evening without succumbing to the temptations of strange women in London.

These two categories of people will find that the House is surprisingly forgiving, since most of the other MPs will be thinking 'there but for the grace of God'. Still, the next time they go in to make a speech or ask a question, it is a good idea to surround them with sympathetic colleagues on your side. This will be much easier for an MP who has been libelled, obviously, and he'll probably get some sympathy even from the other side, most of whom will realise that it could happen to them. If someone has done something foolish but has been set up, you will have to hope that he's popular with the parliamentary party. If they like him, they will take the view that 'he may have been a prat but he's our prat' and give him their support. If he has spent his time being rude to colleagues and denigrating their achievements, they will enjoy his downfall as much as the press. You can only appeal to their loyalty to the party and the need not to give the other side scalp. This usually works with most people, unless someone is very unpopular indeed, in which case they should probably be thinking about retirement.

Your real problem will lie with people who are involved in what they will describe as a 'serious' relationship with someone other than their wives. In the real world, the rows and recriminations usually happen behind closed doors. It's horrible for the people concerned but at least they do not have to work out their family tragedy in the full glare of publicity. The MP concerned will have to decide between his wife and his mistress, if his wife even wants to hang on to him after his misbehaviour. Do not, whatever you do, try to push him in one direction or another. The people involved must work it out for themselves and you are there to pick up the pieces afterwards. The late Robin Cook was famously told to choose between his wife and his secretary (who later became his second wife) on the way to the airport. If anyone is going to push someone into a decision like this, it will be done way above your pay grade and you should be thankful, for it will probably, as in that case, provoke recriminations that will go on for years. Try to keep everyone away from the press, get the erring MP some support from his friends and await the outcome. What you are witnessing is a personal tragedy, but it is not likely to have any long-term effect on the government because no parliamentary rules have been broken. From time to time, the opposition will try to concoct some sort of allegation so that they can debate the issue in Parliament, as they did in Robin's case, but it never gets very far. It simply pushes the erring MP's colleagues into rallying round him and makes the other side look small-minded and opportunistic. It will greatly add to the gaiety of the nation, as they see hammering MPs as a sport akin to bear-baiting and treat them in a way they would never treat their own friends and neighbours, but it won't change anything that matters. What it will do is increase the pressure on the MP, his wife and family, who will be subject to abuse in the press and, even worse, on the internet. The best advice in these situations is never to read the press or look at the online comments but, however much someone knows in their head that this is the right thing to do, their emotions will make them behave otherwise. No one can resist looking, either because they want to know the worst or because they are desperately searching for one supportive comment. There won't be any and they will feel ten times worse. Some people will have their family around to support them or good friends who will stick by them. This is the time when MPs find out who their friends really are and they are often shocked by who sticks by them and who rushes for the exit as fast as possible, claiming to never have known them well.

You should watch out for the loners; those who have never mixed much but, rather, have hidden away in their offices, people who go back to their flats every night to sit on their own and brood. There are a surprising number of people like that in Parliament, far more people who are shy and lonely than the public would expect, and it is these who often get into trouble. The press and the public baiting them for their mistakes never consider that there is a human being on the receiving end, never think that all of us make mistakes in life and that someone at the other end of their tirades might be deeply regretting what they have done and hurting. The internet has made it much easier for people, under the cover of anonymity, to make outrageous and usually untrue accusations about anyone, with no fear of any repercussions. For a person in a fragile emotional state, this can be devastating and the great fear of all Whips' Offices in the middle of a crisis is that one day someone will fail to arrive in the Commons and then be found dead in their flat. It's important, then, that you arrange some emotional support for these people and you will find many other MPs, again contrary to what the public believe, to be surprisingly kind-hearted. This is not because they condone what has happened, but because they understand better than anyone else the pressure that their colleague is under. People will invite him to eat with them or to come for a drink and surround him with a protective cocoon, often without prompting. If that isn't happening, a word from you to a couple of decent souls will usually ensure that it does. The MP concerned will at least be cheered to find that colleagues who he has previously not had much contact with are willing to help him out. It's a small hope to cling on to in a very bad time.

When money is involved, MPs are likely to take a very different view, and so are the press, hence the important whips' question. Sex scandals will come and go, but MPs who are on the fiddle get no sympathy, again contrary to what the public believe. The anger of their colleagues will increase if the MP concerned has been guilty of hypocrisy. That's the reason why most MPs, other than the Lib Dems, have never forgiven David Laws for the scandal over his expenses and think his punishment was far too light. He had put out election leaflets not only claiming to live in the constituency, but boasting that his expenses were the lowest in the area.

The 'expenses scandal', as it was called (despite the fact that for the majority of MPs there was no scandal), threw up some good examples of how MPs view these things. They had real sympathy for those being attacked by the press who, they believed, had done nothing wrong. When articles were written that managed to imply that MPs had claimed for improvement to their flats which they had actually paid for themselves, or berated them for claiming for reasonable articles like a chair (A chair! How dare they want something to sit on!), they received only sympathy from their colleagues. Yet, when they felt that someone had been abusing the system, MPs were as bitter as anyone outside Parliament.

One day, there will no doubt be several theses written about the way the press behaved, how some people who made outrageous claims remained untouched, why some people were pilloried for no reason and how articles were carefully written to imply wrongdoing when there was none, as papers relied on the belief that no MP would dare to sue in the climate of those days. Some future political analyst might even examine why governments raised allowances because they were too afraid to deal with salaries, and how an allowances system

morphed into a hybrid of allowances and expenses, thus causing confusion and ultimate chaos. But that's enough of that!

Two cases will serve to illustrate the difference. One is
the case of Ian Gibson, then MP for Norwich North. Ian had
bought a flat, as he was allowed to do under the rules at the
time, and claimed the interest on his mortgage. Eventually,
he sold the flat to his daughter, allegedly for less than it was
worth. For this, he was pilloried in the press and called before
a panic-stricken Labour Party National Executive Committee.
The story ended with his resignation, fed-up at the way he had
been treated, and the loss of the seat in a by-election, where
Labour was not helped by the fact that we had got rid of an
MP who was fairly popular with his voters.

Ian had broken no rules and the only person who had lost
money was him. Somehow, when making less money than
you might have done on the sale of a flat becomes an offence,
MPs were not impressed with the outcome.

The second case involved a number of MPs who were claiming for mortgages which they didn't have, including some
whose names shocked their fellow MPs. People believed, quite
rightly, that you couldn't simply forget that you had paid off
your mortgage. It is a big event in anyone's life. So they had
very little sympathy for those 'absent-minded' people who
seem to have thought that it made no difference to their claims.
They were even more annoyed that all of them were taking the
flak for what a few people had done.

Unfortunately, in cases like this, there is a tendency for
people not to recognise the trouble they are in. I had to ring

one colleague who featured in the papers over his mortgage claims and found out that he was in the USA, blithely continuing with his trip.

'Do you think he should come back?' his wife asked quietly.

I resisted the temptation to scream down the phone.

'Yes, I do. Straight away,' I replied quietly.

He returned as I asked, but still seemed to think he could avoid trouble. He may well have carried on thinking like that until he was charged.

What you certainly will not want if you face a crisis like this (and I hope you never will) is for senior ministers to come down and lecture their colleagues on appropriate behaviour and the need to show contrition. MPs do not like being told this by members of the Cabinet who earn far more than they do, or by people who have outside interests. Most MPs live on their parliamentary salary. It's a good wage by most people's standards but for many it is less than they would be earning if they'd stuck to their previous jobs. A standard response to a school pupil's question 'How much do you earn?', fired at all MPs, is: 'Less than your head teacher.' Most of the people they deal with – like secondary head teachers, senior local government officers and council chief executives – earn much more than they do. They live with this, but they won't live with people on higher salaries telling them to show contrition, and that includes members of the Cabinet.

Keep these people away from the tea room if you can, even if you can't (and won't) keep them off the airwaves. Senior people in government and opposition have the same reaction to any financial crisis. They vie with one another to show how tough they are being on their own MPs. They promise emergency measures, they vow to bring forward emergency legislation. That is why we have the Independent Parliamentary Standards Authority (IPSA), a system so expensive to run and so complex that is costs millions every year to deliver expenses for 650 MPs, not all of whom can claim under every category. No private business would ever tolerate such a wasteful and torturous system, but it is the result of panic legislation. MPs hate it not, as most people think, because it published their expenses, but because it wastes hours of their time in a system so Byzantine that many claims cost more to process than they are actually worth.

The system was forced through by the leadership of both main parties, with Cabinet ministers descending from on high to tell MPs that they had to show contrition for their sins. The usual reaction from backbenchers was, 'I didn't play the property market.'

They knew that some Cabinet ministers had, perfectly legally, moved a number of times to more expensive flats, making money each time they sold and moved on. Most people, who just wanted a place to live when they were in London and who didn't move unless they had to, found being lectured in this way offensive. Try to keep the two sides apart if you can. Your troops will be feeling bad enough without someone driving them to think of murder.

At times like this, you will have to patrol the House constantly. One of the things the public don't see at a time like this is the despair and the depression that set in among MPs, not because they have done something wrong, but because they haven't. The innocent suffer most because they are assumed guilty, and their families suffer too. During the expenses crisis, wives and husbands were spat at in the supermarket and their children were bullied in the school playground. It's no wonder, given this treatment of their families, that some people decided to leave.

If you spot anyone heading for trouble, try to get them home for a few days (though not if their wife or partner is screaming at them to leave). If you can't give them a break, listen to their troubles. You will have heard it all before, but they need to tell someone. Most people right themselves eventually and everything passes, but even MPs going through a crisis will need a friend. They are only human, even if the public are reluctant to admit this.

Chapter 14

How to stay sane

THERE ARE THOSE who will argue that accepting a job in the Whips' Office is, in itself, proof of insanity, and there are days when you will probably agree with them. When you have arrived at work at eight o'clock, have been running round all day either to secure votes or to avert a crisis, when you have not had time to eat a proper meal and find yourself struggling home at eleven, then you will fall into your flat, discover you have no food there and the milk has gone sour and curse the day you said 'thank you' to the Prime Minister when he offered you the job. Your role puts you under impossible pressure, yet you will have to deal with it. The demands on you are unrelenting and seem to occupy you twenty-four hours a day. You will get phone calls late at night and in the early morning, and they will not stop when you are on holiday. Still, you are there and you have to do the work, so it will be necessary to find some way of keeping yourself from starting to mutter in the street, seeing conspiracies round every corner (except when they really are there) and driving your family insane.

The first thing you need to accept is that you will have to learn to live with tiredness. To be a whip is to be constantly overworked and short of sleep. You will just have to manage this so it doesn't get too out of hand and that means taking every opportunity, however brief, to relax or catch up on sleep. If you are not on bench duty and there are no votes, go back to your flat early, read a book and have an early night (i.e. get to bed before midnight). Leaving early, for you, will mean going at eight o'clock in the evening, but it is better than normal and you need those extra hours.

But how do you stay sane and keep your temper while all this is going on? The answer is simple. You need to find something else to do. In the words that agony aunts have used for over a century, you need a hobby.

You may think that this is impossible. After all, your time is already fully occupied. There are not enough hours in the day to do what you already have to do. How can you possibly fit in anything else? Yet you can – and you will. Trying to do your job as a whip and to get through all your constituency work will mean that you are already working an eighty-hour week, perhaps even more in the bad times. No one in your constituency

will believe this, of course. The general view is that MPs do no
work but just occasionally swan into the Chamber to shout
at the other side. Generally, they are thought to be hanging
about down in London waiting for constituents to drop in
and be given a tour of the House of Commons, treated to tea
on the terrace and introduced to well-known people before
they slope off back to the bars where they spend most of their
time. You may find this view irritating, but there is no point
in complaining about it or trying to correct it, except when
explaining to constituents that you are not available to personally conduct them around the House. Suggest that you actually
do work long hours and people will accuse you of whining
and possibly even point out that they pay your wages so you
damn well should be working. You will not convince anyone
to change this view by working yourself into the ground and
becoming ill. More importantly, as far as the Whips' Office is
concerned, you will not make a very good whip.

So you must carve out some time for yourself when you can
to do things that are not political. This doesn't include cleaning your house, since these extra activities should be things
you actually enjoy. It took me years in Parliament before I gave
in and admitted to myself that finishing work at lunchtime
on a Saturday, or even later, and then spending the rest of the
weekend cleaning and tidying, was not a healthy lifestyle. I had
been brought up on the strict injunction that people should
clear up their own mess. Yet even I had to give in and take on
a cleaner. Most male MPs can skip this bit as they already have
someone to deal with this, known as a 'wife', and they tend

not to notice dirt as much as women do anyway. If you take on a cleaner, just make sure that you pay them properly, that they have a clear contract and that their tax, national insurance and holiday pay are all taken care of. If you can't face doing all this, and most of us can't, then go to a firm who will deal with all that and just send the cleaner to your house. The same advice holds good for MPs' wives, or even, very occasionally, their husbands, who take on the thankless task of finding someone to clean their house. Do not pay cash in hand without a receipt, whatever you do. You're meant to be making laws, not encouraging people to break them.

So, assuming you have the basics of running a house covered, how do you manage to find some spare time? You must carve out a space during the week when you do things that you and your family, if you have one, would like to do. Make sure that there is one day in the week when you don't have constituency engagements. For me, this has always been Sunday. Other than Remembrance Day, I very seldom accept Sunday engagements. People do understand this, because I tell them that it is the day I keep for my family. My family would dispute this assertion since I often spend the time dealing with paperwork or writing speeches, but the important thing is that there is some time in the week over which I have control. Give yourself a slow start, potter about. Yes, you will have to catch up on the household jobs you don't get time to do otherwise (contrary to popular opinion, MPs also have to eat, cook and repair things) but at least you are not doing politics. It is almost impossible for any politician not to read the

Sunday papers, but you should certainly not watch the political programmes. You are meant to be getting away from the job and if anyone says anything really stupid or interesting, you will soon be told.

Your free time may be different depending on the demands of your constituency, but once you have carved out some time in the week, what you do with it is up to you. Some people take up walking but for me it was gardening that worked. I'm not a particularly good gardener but being outside for an hour or two on a Sunday, in the fresh air and doing something completely different from politics, allowed me to switch off and keep some sense of perspective. A surprising number of MPs take to gardening simply because it is so different from politics. 'You can't rush a garden,' as one of my colleagues said with satisfaction. Others go off to see their local football team (note: going to the directors' box where people want to talk politics to you does not count). Others decide to take themselves off to the theatre or the opera during the week or on a Saturday afternoon. It really doesn't matter what you choose to do as long as you go off and do something different. Preferably, do something that gets you outside. You are stuck in Parliament all day when it is sitting. When you are back in your constituency you are rushing between visits and other engagements. You need a complete change.

Yes, you will say, but there are other things I have to do. No doubt there are, but you won't be able to do them all, so decide what has to be neglected. All women MPs, in my experience, worry about the state of their house. Men don't notice things like that. Just decide to do the basics and leave it at that. There were new life forms evolving in the back of my fridge by the time the 2010 election was over, but it eventually got cleared out and no one suffered, so try to concentrate on the things that are important. Similarly, many MPs obsess about the amount of paperwork they have and devote a large chunk of their Sunday to it. Don't. Lots of people will send you things but *you do not have to read it all.* Ask your staff to put aside things that are important to your constituency, or that relate to your special interest. You should try to keep up with these because you won't always be a whip, but accept that you will not be as knowledgeable or up to date as you once were. Then throw the rest away. Really. That's what the bin is for. If possible, get your staff to throw it away so you are not tempted to even start to read it. That way madness lies. Whatever you do, do not work on these things on a Sunday. Read them on the train to London, or put them aside for when you have half an hour to spare during your working day and go back to your own office. You need to take charge of the paperwork before it takes over your life.

You also need the occasional day out. Sometimes you will find there is a day when you are free. These are exceptionally rare but you need to make use of them when you can. Do not be tempted to fill them up with extra paperwork, to clean out the fridge or to do any of the other jobs you have been putting off. You have put them off for the very good reason that they are not essential, so you don't need to do them now. Go out to lunch with your family. Drive out for a walk in the country or by the sea. Whatever you do, get away from your constituency. You do not want your office ringing you up to ask about casework, to speak to you about invitations or anything else that is not urgent, so tell them you are taking a day off, or, if you don't want them to know, say that you're ill in bed and should only be disturbed in an emergency. Then leave. Don't hang about – just go.

The one thing you cannot do, unfortunately, is to switch your mobile off. Whips are never off-duty and the Chief or the Deputy will not be happy if they try to get hold of you and you are not answering. Anyone else can be disregarded. Cough alarmingly and tell them you'll get back to them when you feel better or just don't answer the call and, if they leave a message, do not listen to it until you get home. You need time out.

Some people find it useful to have something to do with their hands (no, not the things that get you in the papers). I used to do cross-stitch and knitting simply to help me relax in the evening but, if you do take up anything like this, try to keep it in the privacy of your own home. You do not want to sit in the Whips' Office looking like a Victorian maiden at work. It will not sit well with your reputation as a really hard case. There must be a male equivalent of this somewhere but it's hard to imagine what it is. Woodwork can't be carted about and doesn't have the same effect on people.

One thing you should never do is to read political books. Some people seem to think it is compulsory to keep up with all the latest theories and political biographies. It isn't and most of them are rubbish anyway. Read fiction, or non-fiction that is not about politics, and always have at least one book on the go. I used to mix up serious stuff with easy reading and, if I was very tired, I'd switch to the easy stuff. There's nothing like a good murder to get you off to sleep at night.

Whatever you decide to do, if you are a whip, you have to be prepared for interruptions from time to time. Sometimes what you have planned to do will be cancelled. Sometimes, you will be interrupted by one of your flock who does not take the hint to ring you back another time. I still cherish the memory of the MP who rang me when I was on holiday and, when told where I was, continued the conversation anyway. You can't turn your phone off (although you better make sure you have it on silent in the theatre, opera or concerts unless you want to make yourself very unpopular) but you just have to take the risk and get on. Doing something different will refresh your mind and your body and make you much more able to cope with the stress you face day after day. You may think you are indispensable, but there are plenty of indispensable people in the cemetery. What you choose to do doesn't matter too much (although it is advisable to avoid recreations that will get you on the front pages of the tabloids) as long as you do something purely for enjoyment.

The other important thing is to keep in touch with your friends, both inside and outside Parliament. You will have friends who are ministers and others on the back benches, but make time to see them at some point in the week. Join them for a coffee or sit down and have a meal in the dining room with them and don't, above all, try to be a whip while you're there. Make it clear that you are off-duty, chat about anything that comes up, say that you are not there to be harangued about whatever government policy has upset them that week. If they really are your friends, they will understand the pressures you are under and allow you the luxury of a bit of time off.

Most politicians have friends outside Parliament (yes, really!) but not many of them are outside the political arena. Many will be members of their own political party who they have met, just as others do, through their work. Most of these people are good to spend time with because you have a shared history and a shared set of assumptions. If you have known them for a long time, there are things you don't have to waste time explaining. They will know when you are tired and they will have at least some idea of the demands of your job. However, being political activists, they will also be avid for the latest gossip from Westminster and that is just what you can't tell them. Make it clear from the start that discretion in a whip is absolute and must extend even to your friends. Not that you believe that they would be indiscreet of course, perish the thought, but someone else might be. Good friends will understand this and will welcome your company without expecting you to sing for your supper.

If you know people with whom you've always pursued a hobby, or gone for a drink with or have kept in touch with since you left school, you should cherish them. These are the people who will keep your feet firmly on the ground. They don't care much about the latest Westminster gossip, or who's up and who's down. They don't suck up to you simply because you might have some influence. They're your mates and you are lucky to have them, so make sure that you keep in touch even if the job means that you can't always spend as much time with them as you would like. You won't always have the job, but you can hope to keep your friends.

Your family, of course, you can never get rid of. Your immediate family, your partner and children, are your greatest supporters and the best people at bringing you down to earth with a bang. 'Gran said you were very good on the telly,' my son said to me once when he was a child.

'Was I?' I asked.

'Don't know,' was the response. 'I was watching Star Trek on the other side.'

There is nothing better than a small child for showing you your place in the scheme of things.

If you are lucky enough to have an extended family – aunts, uncles, cousins and so on – they will undoubtedly drive you mad at times. They will boast about you to their neighbours, expect that you can solve problems where they live and be cross when you tell them that you can't because it's not your constituency. The older ones will, like any family, continue to treat you as if you are still five. When not talking to people outside, they will, no doubt, imply that their own offspring have done better than you because they have 'proper jobs'. They do all this because they are family and you should be grateful because when a crisis strikes, whether it's a flood in your house, a sudden illness or a horrible article in the press, they will be the ones who stand by you. Like your old friends, they value you because of who you are, not what you've achieved, so be thankful for them, go to family parties, remember their birthdays, play with the small children and be glad you have what many people crave – a group of people who will fight with you, tell you where you've gone wrong and love you, because you're one of them.

I hope you are beginning to see a pattern in what I'm saying here. Politics is an overwhelming part of your life, as it should be if you're a whip, but it must not be the whole of your life. If you allow it to become so you will lose all sense of perspective and, not only will your judgement be poor but, when you are sacked (as everyone is eventually, remember), you will be one of those sad souls who does not know what to do with themselves. Being a government whip is so time-consuming, so all-encompassing and, let's be honest, so much fun sometimes, that it is difficult to imagine doing anything else, but you must not only imagine it, but do it. Life is not a dress rehearsal. Good whips know this so remember your friends and family, do things that aren't political and stay balanced, in so far as you can. Among my fellow whips there were people who went to the opera, avid Shakespeare-watchers, people who escaped to their caravan or walking in the lakes – all the best whips knew when it was time for a breather. They were also the most hard-working and the most reliable in a crisis. Granted, we kept our cultured side well-hidden as we did not want to damage our reputation as a bunch of thugs, but we still needed these things to keep us sane. Find what works for you and do it.

The best way of keeping sane comes from having that sense of perspective. I learnt this the hard way during the expenses crisis. Life was awful. Like all MPs, I was receiving my share of abusive letters and emails. I did not know which of my colleagues would be attacked next. People I knew who had done no wrong and had not been accused of doing wrong wished to leave Parliament because they feared the effect the scandal would have on their families. Others were being told that they faced divorce if they stood for Parliament again. Wives and husbands had simply had enough. I hated going to the shops because I knew I would get the same comment every time: 'Are you putting that on expenses?' One MP told me that his wife, out doing the weekly shop, had been spat at in the supermarket. He had not been accused of any wrongdoing. I didn't think I could take much more.

Then, one day, a young woman made an appointment to see me. She could not come to the normal surgery and none of my male staff could be in the room. The reason was both simple and horrific. She had been violently raped. What is more, she had been badly let down afterwards by all the agencies that should have helped her. She had been sent back to her flat where her bed and parts of her bedroom were covered in blood. No counselling was offered to her. She was unable to go to work and had not been given any benefits. The local housing trust either would not or could not offer her any alternative accommodation. Her parents had had to travel from another part of the country to try to assist their daughter, who was alone in a town where she knew few people. The full details of what had happened to her were so horrific that I cannot write them here in case it leads to her being identified.

Fortunately, she belonged to a church in another town whose members had been offering her help and support and wanted to continue that help. Could she possibly be moved to live nearer to them? It seemed a very modest request in the circumstances and I assured her that I would do my best to arrange it. My staff went in to action to get her benefits sorted out and, with the help of another local council, we were able to arrange a move for her. I never discovered what happened to her after that or whether her attacker was caught and sentenced.

I hope she made a new life for herself, for she was a very courageous young woman and her visit taught me a very valuable lesson. Whatever pressure MPs were under and however hard it was working in the Whips' Office at that time, there were people in far more difficult circumstances than us, people in real pain, people undergoing privations that we can hardly imagine. Whenever I am tempted to bemoan my lot, I think of that young woman and remember that, however bad things get, I am hugely privileged. Keeping a sense of perspective is the key to holding on to your sanity. Whatever happens, you are still better off than most of the people on this planet. You have food and a warm home, your children can go to school, and you do not have to trek for miles to find clean water. Even if you look at your own constituency, you will find people who struggle to make ends meet, people working at several part-time jobs to keep their families going, those coping with long-term illness or caring for relatives who are ill. You are blessed compared to them and you should try to remember it.

You will also bear this in mind when someone emails or writes to you or attends your surgery with a trivial complaint. Leaves falling on their lawn from someone else's tree or children playing football spring to mind. You will be tempted to try to give them a sense of perspective too, especially now poverty is growing and people are losing their jobs, their benefits and often their homes. Don't do it unless you are planning on retiring soon. 'Here is a list of all the other things I have had to deal with today,' may give you great satisfaction but it won't work with your constituents who always believe that their problem is the greatest in the world. Nor is it advisable to use this as a way of trying to console the Chief Whip if you lose a vote. 'Ah well, there's always someone worse off,' is not a response to give if you want to stay in your job. Just keep it in your own mind and focus on it when things get tough.

Chapter 15

Keeping your
constituents happy

I T USED TO be said that an MP in a marginal seat
should never become a whip, although a number
of them did and still do. The reasoning behind that
advice was simple. Whips cannot show dissent,
they cannot vote against the government unless they are
willing to resign and they cannot make speeches. Since
nowadays the effectiveness of MPs is often measured by
how much they speak (rather than whether what they say
is of any use), this can be a real handicap to being seen as
a good constituency MP. Your voting record will go up but,

on sites like They Work For You, you will be shown as not having spoken.

So, if you are going to be a whip and you want to be re-elected, you have to find ways to make the job work for you in the constituency. First and foremost, do not neglect your constituency. However tired you are at the end of the week, however many late nights you have had, you will still be expected to do the normal round of constituency visits and campaigning on Fridays and Saturdays. You will get no sympathy at all, since most of your constituents have no idea of the hours you work, so don't expect any. Look cheerful and interested and try not to yawn too much. If you do, for heaven's sake remember to explain (briefly) that you are not yawning because a constituent is boring you, but because you haven't had much sleep. They will, however, still ask you if you have to go to London often. Curb your impatience: these are the people you want to vote for you.

You will also find that people are surprisingly pleased when their constituency MP gets promoted. They see it as reflecting their own good judgement in picking you, so feel free to tell them about your good fortune without going over the top. Remember that you won't be there for ever. They are also interested in what whips do. It's one of the areas of Parliament that people know very little about so tell them how it works. I took to including little snippets on newsletters about what a whip does and was surprised by the reaction I got. Most people found it interesting to know, but you can only get away with this if the rest of your publication is filled with what you are doing for the voters of Anytown. Do not for one minute let them think that your work in the Whips' Office is more important than they are. It isn't. After all, without them you wouldn't be there.

So, you will need to make sure that no one notices any change in the level of your efforts within the constituency. Photo calls, visits to local schools, your local hospital and other worthy organisations must continue as usual. In my constituency, we also had a tradition of holding 'mobile surgeries', which is a fancy way of saying knocking on people's doors to talk to them and ask if they have any problems or issues they would like to raise. People liked this, although I have to say that despite the fact that I have done this almost every week since I was elected (summer holidays and Christmas excepted), people still tell me that politicians only call on them at election time.

However you organise your campaigning, you must keep it up. People will not forgive you if they think you have deserted them for the bright lights and fleshpots of London and you will get nowhere by telling them that your bright lights and fleshpots consist of a crowded Whips' Office with the occasional packet of biscuits on offer. You will not be able to get away early on a Thursday as many of your colleagues look forward to doing, and you will have to be present on some Fridays when the House is dealing with Private Members' Bills, although most Whips' Offices arrange a rota and have abandoned the practice of having a 'Friday whip' who got lumbered with them all.

As your time in the constituency will be more limited, you must make the best use of it and, in my view, this means using it to contact voters. Many MPs spend too much time with the 'great and the good' of their area. Many of these people probably do not live in your constituency and often would not vote for you if they did. Council officers continually want to organise meetings to 'brief' you on certain things. This is to validate their existence rather than to help you keep your job. Be ruthless. Instruct your staff to cut down on the meetings, ask for briefings in writing and only see those people you really want to see. Cut back on the round of events for the high and mighty and get out among your voters instead. I abandoned most of these soon after the 1997 election when I realised that I was meeting the same people over and over again and that few of them lived in Warrington North.

What you should aim for is at least one event that will get your picture in the local paper and one session of voter contact each Friday, whether it's knocking on doors, hosting a 'tea with your MP' session, visiting sheltered accommodation, or whatever else you can come up with. Regular appearances in your local paper are essential and are best achieved by the assiduous pursuit of local issues. Once they have announced your promotion, the paper will not be interested in what you are doing in London.

To achieve all this you will need good, reliable staff who can organise your diary without you constantly giving them instructions. Hopefully, by the time you are made a whip, you will have a settled staff in your constituency office who can get on with the job. Mine used to give me my Friday and Saturday diary on a Thursday and I would just turn up and do it. The one thing you should insist on is that you have some time in to deal with your constituency post and to talk to your staff. Letters from constituents are important and should be responded to as soon as possible. You will find that staff who are used to your methods can prepare the answers to many of them without speaking to you but you should always try to sign them personally. Others may need some discussion if they raise a difficult issue or one that no one has dealt with before. Sit down and go through the post with your staff each week, being clear about how you want the letters to be dealt with. Talk through plans for the next few weeks, where you should be visiting, who has asked to see you and so on so that you can all decide which things are the most important. Good staff will also recognise when you are getting too exhausted and arrange a slightly quieter day for you. It's not in their interests for you to be in a state where you're making a mess of things because you are so tired you can't think straight. However, the definition of exhaustion for an MP is not the same as for others. Constant tiredness goes with the job. Only when you're finding it almost impossible to drag yourself to the next appointment will you be told to slack off a bit. Besides, they will be worried about your pictures in the local paper looking dreadful.

Assiduous work on constituency cases can generate you a lot of publicity and good will but, since you can no longer ask questions or join in debates, you cannot raise issues on the floor of the House as you used to. Instead, you will have to write to ministers or ask for a meeting with them. Make sure that they give you a decent answer to any queries you have raised and that they meet you if you request it. There is an unwritten, but strictly enforced, rule that ministers should always respond positively to a request for a meeting from a whip for two reasons. The first is that you are a fellow minister; the second that you have no other way of raising a constituency issue.

If you don't get a quick response, stop the minister in the lobby and ask why. The likelihood is that he or she will not have seen your letter, which has disappeared somewhere in the bowels of the ministry's correspondence unit. Ask for a quick reply, or for a meeting if you want one. You will then be able to tell your constituent, or the local press if it is an issue that affects lots of people, that you have met the minister to discuss the problem. It is even better if the minister agrees to some action and, even if you can't get all you want, you should always try to come out of a meeting having made some progress. 'MP meets minister and nothing happens' is not a good headline and makes people think you are totally useless. If you can't get a result when you are in the Whips' Office, they will be right.

Most ministers will try to meet you and do what they can to help with constituency problems because they understand the situation you are in. They also know that you can make their lives very difficult if they refuse to assist you. If anyone is really uncooperative, you should tell one of the senior whips, who will ensure that the office protects its own. Often a word from the Chief or the Deputy is enough to get you what you are asking for but, if that doesn't work, you should get the office to go into full non-cooperation mode. Revenge tactics can include scheduling statutory instrument committees for that minister at the most inconvenient times (late on Thursday afternoon or at 8.55 a.m. are the favourites for this), refusing requests for time away from the House, and making sure that any request to leave early during the evening is turned down. You will need the help of the pairing whip and the whip in charge of statutory instruments to do this but you will find they are more than willing to help you. Remember, in the Whips' Office, an injury to one is an injury to all.

If that doesn't work, you can try putting very unhelpful people who ask awkward questions onto any committee they have to deal with, although you will need to see that there are enough people there for the government to win the vote. Ministers may complain about all of these tactics, but should be told that cooperation is a two-way street and that the office will be very helpful to the minister the minute they start being helpful to you. Most don't bother. They soon get the message, give you a meeting or send the letter you have been asking for and normal service will resume.

All of these things will help you keep up your constituency profile but you must make sure that you never over-claim about what you can deliver. Saying that you can take Anytown's concerns straight to a minister is one thing, promising that you can deliver more money, new schools or anything else is likely to get you into serious trouble. Government doesn't work like that and sensible ministers who wish to survive in the Whitehall jungle make sure that they take decisions on a proper basis. One MP appointed as a very lowly ministerial bag-carrier promised that she could deliver more investment for her town because she was now in the Treasury. Of course, she couldn't, and the pledge was seen to be a bit of idle boasting. Don't allow yourself to fall into that trap, but do remember that your constituency comes first. Many members of government have forgotten that in the past and have found themselves no longer ministers because their constituents didn't re-elect them.

Your local paper will also appreciate a visit to the government Whips' Offices, both in the House and in Downing Street. These are places local reporters and photographers don't often get invited to and it gives them the chance of a day in London. Don't do this too soon, but wait until you have got your feet under the table so that you can show them around and explain what is happening. They will be struck by how unglamorous everything is and this will reinforce your constituents' belief in your hard work. They particularly enjoy being taken over to the Downing Street office, where pictures of former whips line the walls. If you are lucky, you will get a nice page of pictures and accompanying text in the paper the following week. Just remember several points. Do not take them into the daily whips' meeting or your colleagues will be horrified and you will feel stupid as they are ushered out. Make sure the other whips know they are coming so that they don't leave anything confidential on their desks, and get the Chief's permission before you show them around his office.

It goes without saying that you will, of course, provide generous refreshments after their long journey. They will be happy, the readers will get a glimpse behind the scenes of government and you can bask in the resulting good publicity. As a bonus, your opponents in the constituency will be furious since they cannot provide the press with anything like that sort of spread. It's one of the few perks of the job.

Chapter 16

Keeping your members happy

SOME MPs WILL say that their party members are never happy, and it is true that you can't keep everyone happy all the time. Yet, while there will always be people who grumble and will never be satisfied whatever you do, most members are on your side and will be happy about your promotion. Like your voters, they will see it as a vindication of their judgement in having selected you. This doesn't mean that you don't need to work at keeping them informed about what your job entails and what you can and cannot do.

Just like the rest of your constituents, many of your members will wonder why you are no longer jumping up to ask questions or make speeches, so it is important that you make clear to them what your job entails. Use your reports to them to explain why you are not allowed to speak any more and exactly how you are responsible for getting legislation through. You can also tell them bits of gossip from the Whips' Office and juicy tit-bits about ministers. One word of warning – keep these light and never, ever put them in a written report. Your rule should be simple: never tell your members anything that you wouldn't want to see in the press. It is a sad truth that there is no such thing as a confidential political meeting: somebody always leaks. By and large, your members will be happy with a little elaboration of stories they have already heard and a few harmless nuggets about why the Prime Minister came in to congratulate the whips and what he said. Do not, under any circumstances, run down other MPs, even if you have good reason to. This applies even if your constituency believe that Mr X is wonderful and you know that he is a lazy toerag who is always messing up in Parliament. The same rule applies in spades if you know someone has money troubles or is cheating on their partner. One word from you and you will have broken the code of omertà which rules the Whips' Office. The comments will be traced back and you will be out on your ear.

Instead, tell your members about the funny bits of procedure you come across and the strange things that happen while you are sitting on the bench. They will feel that they are being taken into your confidence and that they know much more about what is going on than neighbouring constituencies, who are not so fortunate as to have a member in the Whips'

Office. When I was promoted within the Whips' Office, my members were delighted to hear about the fact that I had to write to the Queen every day and that I was the person held hostage at the State Opening of Parliament. Many of these things will seem like commonplace chores to you, but to your members, far from Westminster, they are interesting. Don't forget to mention (but not labour) the long hours you work. Most party members are kind people who will actually sympathise as long as you don't go on about it too much. You should also subtly imply that the whole office depends on you to keep the government on the road. Most of the people who selected you want to be proud of you, so let them.

Unfortunately, there will always be a few who do not take this view. Every MP knows that there are always people around who think they can do the job better than you can, or who feel that you have an easy life which they deserve much more than you do. They will be the people who jump up in party meetings demanding that you vote against the government on whatever issue of concern is currently in their minds and they will complain if you miss any local event, however small, even if you weren't actually invited to it.

The way to deal with these people is not to confront them but to enlist the sympathy of others. Tell your members that when you took on your job, loyalty was required whatever happened. You knew that when you accepted and so did they. They wouldn't expect you to break your word and you are not going to do so. Remember that most of your members are loyalists who want the government to succeed, so remind them of that loyalty. You are not there to be divisive, you can tell them, but to ensure your party wins. You will not be giving aid and comfort to the opposition and they wouldn't expect you to. Remember that some of your members will be councillors who have to abide by the decisions of their group. Often you will find that the person asking you to lead the rebellion is a councillor who would never tolerate the same behaviour from their own colleagues, so remind them of this. They've asked for it.

The best way to prevent anyone challenging for your seat is to make sure that you have a good record as a constituency MP, as discussed previously. If you are looking after your patch well, then anyone challenging you will look so obviously self-seeking that they will get very little sympathy from anyone else. Try to ignore them while making sure that you know what they are up to at any time. You are a whip, after all. You should tip off your loyalists that so-and-so is after your seat as this usually makes them very angry and ensures that they watch the offender closely, but don't go on about it too much or you will look insecure. If someone really becomes a nuisance, a quiet word about (if you are a Labour MP) the number of trade union branches you have on your side (for some reason they seldom count these) and how damaging it will be to their future prospects to try to deselect a sitting MP may become necessary. The best approach, however, is simply to repeat the old Harold Wilson saying, 'I know what's going on. I am going on.'

You should also ensure that your members enjoy some of the perks that your office can bring them. You will be much better placed to get senior ministers to visit your constituency, especially if they are indebted to you for time off. Your members will enjoy mingling with those in power and, of course, the ministers will tell them how wonderful you are. This is an absolute requirement for anyone visiting another MP's constituency and people do it on auto-pilot. However, your members do not know this and will believe that the words are fresh-minted just for you and they will congratulate themselves once again for having seen your potential at the selection conference.

If you are lucky, you will also have access to gifts that cannot be obtained elsewhere. One year, the Prime Minister's PPS brought into the office a list of gifts available from the No. 10 shop, which can only be used by people who work there. The whips put in a shipping order, which she duly carried over, and our party members were delighted to be getting their Christmas gifts direct from No. 10. Even if they just got a mug, they were getting something that couldn't be bought elsewhere and were left with the impression that we, and by extension they, had privileged access.

The one thing that your members will enjoy most, though, is a visit to the Downing Street Whips' Office. Just like your local press, they will love to go to a place where few people ever get to tour and will be very grateful to you for arranging it for them. So, if you ever have a group visiting London, try to get permission to take them around. Most Chief Whips realise the value of this to members of their office and will be happy to give you permission to arrange it, but don't make the promise until you have got his or her agreement as you never know what might be going on in Downing Street that day. If the American President is visiting, no one will get in and it can be difficult if other Heads of State are around. You may have to time your visit so as not to clash with theirs. Sadly, No. 10 and the Foreign Office will not see a visit from your constituency members as more important than that of a Head of State. These people just have a skewed sense of priorities simply because they do not have to get reselected and then re-elected.

First, make sure that you have a list of the names of all your visitors and that you have cleared it with security. They will not be impressed if they are kept outside the gates because they are not on the visitors' list and you will look not so much like an efficient whip as a complete prat. When you get people inside, remember that what is commonplace to you will seem remarkable to them, so be prepared for them to stand gazing at the pictures of past Whips' Offices on the walls of the corridor and equip yourself with a few interesting pieces of information about some of them. Let them see the old wall of Whitehall Palace, which is inside the building, and explain how the buildings all connect up with one another. Take them into the room where whips have their weekly meetings and let them sit around the table while you tell them about it. You can even, with permission, let them have a peek into the Chief Whip's office. If you are lucky and the Chief is about, he will say a few words of welcome and tell them all how wonderful you are. Don't try to prevent this: he is your boss. Just remember not to disturb the civil servants who are at work in the building and to keep your group together. You are in a high-security area and the last thing you want is people wandering off and trying doors that they are not allowed to go through. A visit is not improved by armed police appearing and pointing their guns at your members.

People given such a tour will go home and tell their friends all about it, especially if you imply that you have pulled strings to get them into areas where the public are not normally allowed – which you have, in a way. If you are very lucky, the Chief Whip may, as mine once did, arrange a party in Downing Street. This happened one summer as a thank-you to hard-pressed whips and each of us was allowed to bring two people from our constituency. Those who went from mine still talk about it. The only problem you will have is choosing who can go. Either send someone who has done such a remarkable amount of work that no one could quarrel with the choice, or announce that you are putting the names of all your key workers in a hat and drawing two out. Just don't be seen to be playing favourites or those excluded will never forgive you. You can, of course, fiddle the draw as long as no one is there to witness it. After all, I didn't say you *couldn't* play favourites, just that you should not be *seen* to do so.

Your aim in all these things ought to be to make sure that your party members share in your good fortune while not, of course, sharing in your long hours and exhaustion. Remember that you are lucky. Only 650 people can be Members of Parliament at any time, even fewer become ministers. There may not be many perks of the job, but what few there are should be shared with those who put you there by sending you to

Parliament. Show some gratitude and let them enjoy it with you and they will be grateful in return. That means that when someone complains that you cannot make it to a vicarage tea party, they will speak up on your behalf and tell people how busy you are and what a wonderful job you're doing. Everyone benefits, except your opponents and that is as it should be.

Another important advantage is that when you have to go through the reselection process, as we all do, the party machine will be on your side. You may think that this is the case for all MPs. Sadly, it isn't. Political parties are now staffed by people aged about sixteen and a half who have never had a proper job. Unlike the old professional organisers who spent years of their lives working for a pittance, these people do not want to be there for long. Many of them want your job, either for themselves or for a friend, and the many members of their clique scattered throughout the party bureaucracy form a mutually supportive network of the smug and the self-satisfied.

However, they cannot target you while you are a whip. Taking out the Prime Minister's whips is above their pay grade, but that does not mean that you won't have trouble from others. The perennially disaffected and disappointed love reselections. It's the time when they get their revenge for the fact that the constituency did not select them years ago. The idea that they weren't chosen because they were not good enough will never enter their heads. It's your fault. You manipulated the selection, you pulled a fast one (usually by getting more votes than they did), so now it's time for revenge.

You will, of course, face the usual accusations that you are

not in the constituency enough. All MPs face this and sometimes it's true but it's a bit much when you actually live there
and you have been slogging your way around it every weekend
for years. Ignore this. If you've been doing your job, it won't
get any traction.

The other form of attack will be to say that you have sold
out. You are not representing the area anymore because you
can't make speeches or 'speak up' for Anytown. Don't, whatever you do, answer this yourself. Just make sure that you
have someone in each branch where there might possibly be
trouble and get them to tell everyone about your meetings
with ministers and your direct access to the top. You mustn't
boast, but they can, and however often you have explained this
to your General Committee, there will be people in branches
who only turn up every four years for reselections and have
never heard it before. Make sure they are told.

You will also find people who complain that you have never
voted against the government. It is a peculiarity of some party
members that they judge MPs not on how they have supported
their own government, but on when they haven't. Under Tony
Blair, the little bureaucrats in the party made a spectacular
miscalculation when they demanded that a whips' report be
sent out for every reselection, showing how many times an MP
had voted against the government. Far from being a stick to
beat them with, this became a badge of honour for many MPs,
who were able to portray themselves as fiercely independent
and uncorrupted by office, even if they just voted against the
government on a reflex basis.

In the days when you were a humble backbencher, it was useful to have at least one vote against the whip, the reasons for which you had, of course, carefully explained to your local party beforehand. Now, that can't be done, but if you have already explained to your General Committee about the need to keep your word and so on, it will be taken up by other members.

Since you will have the party machine on your side, any infringement of the rules will be pounced on immediately if a branch votes not to reselect you. It is very unlikely that this will happen but, if it does, immediately recheck the list of those present, looking for anyone who is not paid up to date, or find a minor flaw in the procedure and they will have to do it again. By the time a second meeting is arranged you will, I hope, have already won and they won't think it worth voting against you. Of course, you will have dozens of friendly trade union branches affiliated, ready to vote for you. If you haven't, you shouldn't be a whip. Contrary to what most people believe, trade unions do not normally seek to deselect Labour MPs. Conservatives may wish to boast about the support they have from Central Office. You will also have won all, or at least the vast majority, of your party branches. If you haven't, what are you doing in the Whips' Office?

Chapter 17

The top table

AFTER I HAD learnt my trade as a junior whip, there was another reshuffle in 2009. Like everyone else, I awaited the outcome with some trepidation. Was I staying or being sacked? I wasn't expecting promotion, but just hoping to cling on to my job. Reshuffles are great entertainment for those watching them, but hellish for everyone involved. Surprising though it may seem to members of the public, politicians, just like other people, do not enjoy being sacked. Knowing that it will happen to almost everyone in the end is no consolation. Even people who don't like the job they're in would like to go in their own time. So, like everyone else, I waited for the call. None came. It seemed that I'd been completely forgotten. Finally, with a great deal of trepidation, I approached the Chief. Was I staying or going? He looked at me as if it were obvious. 'You're going to be the top woman in the Whips' Office,' he said. So, to no one's surprise except, it seemed, mine, I moved upwards. I became the heir to the magnificent title of Vice-Chamberlain of Her Majesty's Household and one of what was referred to as the 'top table' of the Whips' Office.

Should you ever be offered such a promotion, it's worth knowing that no money comes with it. The Whips' Office is one of the most egalitarian of departments in that everybody, except the Chief Whip and Deputy Chief Whip, gets the same salary. Instead of money you get more work, more responsibilities, earlier starts and more late nights. You also get, if you are the Vice-Chamberlain, the job of writing to the Queen every day that Parliament is in session, a rod of office that looks like a billiard cue, and the job of being held hostage at the palace whenever the Queen comes to open Parliament. You will also be forced (and in my case, 'forced' was the right word) to attend all the summer garden parties.

There are many people who take the job of writing to HMQ, as she is usually called by the civil servants, extremely seriously. When I was appointed, I was shown files of handwritten letters that people had lovingly scribed for Her Majesty and copied for their future edification and, presumably, that of future historians. You do not need to fall into this trap. I am told that the Queen does read the letters and so you should try to make sure that all the relevant information is included, but there is no need to spend hours of your time on them. They are really not that important and future historians will find all the details of that day's business in Hansard. My method was to allow the civil servants to draft that day's 'message' and then to check it and maybe, if I had nothing important to do, add a bit of detail. The civil servants had a competition to see who could do it the fastest. Then, after seeing me correct mistakes, they competed to see who could do it in the shortest time without my correcting it. The competition was won by an English graduate, of course. That is exactly the right attitude. It's a chore and one that has to be done in the shortest time possible. Do not fool yourself into believing that the monarch sits entranced by your carefully crafted words. No doubt that she reads them as part of her job, but drafting them is just a part of your work. Get it out of the way and move on to more important things.

In any case, if you are a senior whip, you certainly do have more important things to do. You are now no longer just responsible for your own work, but for other people's too. Problems will land on your desk repeatedly or arrive via phone calls. When problems arise, it will be your job to solve them and they are certain to arise every day. If you are lucky, they will be small things that you can deal with; on days when you are not so lucky, all your plans will be wrecked. Get used to it: this is your job.

The first thing that you will notice is that you will be at work earlier in the mornings, especially on Wednesdays, when the government whips have their breakfast meetings. You will be used to this beginning at 9 a.m. but, in our office, the senior whips met together at 8.30 a.m. in the Chief Whip's office. In practice, as I discovered, the business begins earlier as people arrive, check the morning papers and try to grab some tea or coffee and a bacon roll before the vultures waiting in the main conference room snatch them all. I got used to these morning meetings, usually arriving yawning desperately after a late night and talking through our troubles with my colleagues before the official business started. Then, with us spread out on the sofas, the Chief would take us through what business was coming up and the problems we faced (which, at that time, were many) and we would discuss the way forward. In the last year of the Labour government, we were happy to get to the end of a week without a crisis and all the news was bad. We would talk it through, desperately trying to find a way forward and venting our frustrations over uncooperative colleagues, disloyal ministers and the general meltdown which was going on all around us. We all felt better for airing our frustrations. You will find it helpful too, even in less trying circumstances. Treat these informal discussions as a therapy session. It is unlikely that you will find a solution to your problems because, usually, there isn't one, but you will feel better for knowing others feel the same way.

There is, however, one rule that you must always abide by. What is said in the Chief's office stays there. You can never repeat what you hear, not even to other whips. You may know what troubles are coming down the line, what was discussed at Cabinet, who the Chief thinks is being disloyal, which ministers are falling out, but you will never be able to say so. Once you walk out of that room it will be as if the conversation has never taken place and you will walk into the main meeting with a smile on your face, looking as if everything is under control. If you don't, you will demoralise everyone. Keep your worries to yourself and act as if everything is going according to plan. This is expected of every whip, but even more so of those at the top table.

You will find that you are also asked to carry more responsibility. Our Chief Whip not only attached me to the Ministry of Justice where he expected, rightly, that there would be plans afoot that would upset the PLP, but put me in charge of statutory instruments. This is a bit like being put in charge of dragging people to the dentist's chair for an operation without anaesthetic. No one wants to do SI committees. It is one of the most boring jobs in Parliament, especially if you are on the government side and therefore not expected to rock the boat. Lots of people will do anything to avoid them and will come up with the most inventive excuses not to be there. My job was to approve the lists of those put on the committees and the scheduling of them. Not only did I need to keep an eye out for anyone who might cause trouble on a particular committee, I also had to disabuse new whips of the idea that they could let people off them. The new members of the office were nice people who were inclined to accept the excuses they were given by those who did not want to turn up to a committee. It had to be gently pointed out to them that the same people were always coming up with excuses. However, after a few weeks of trawling the corridors trying to find replacements for the drop-outs and begging their friends to come to the rescue, they became as hardened and cynical as the rest of us.

It's not enough for you to scrutinise the lists of people appointed to committees and leave it at that. You need to make sure that those committees are running properly and that new whips are not hitting trouble and, yes, that does mean being in early in the morning, making sure that all is in order before the committees start at 8.55. After that, you should take a stroll around the committee corridor, dropping in on the various SIs and sitting at the back for a while watching the proceedings. You should smile at your own whip, especially if they're new, so that they don't think they have committed some terrible mistake that has brought you running up from the office. (Good whips never run, by the way, because they never show panic.) However, a good stare at the opposition whip is always useful as he will get the message that you are keeping an eye on him so that messing one of your newbies about will bring swift retaliation. It's also useful to have a notebook with you so that you can pretend to write things down. You don't actually have to write anything that makes sense, but it keeps both the minister and some of the more ambitious backbenchers on their toes if they think you are reporting back on their performance. Ministers who go on too long should receive the appropriate glares, tuts and shakes of the head to indicate that you believe he or she is a complete prat. This is usually a fair description of anyone who speaks for too long in a committee, which is designed to last no more than an hour and a half and where most of their own backbenchers do not want to be. If they do go on too long, a word when you next happen to meet them about how you have noticed in committees that it is always the most inexperienced ministers who feel obliged to read out every word the civil servants give them usually works, even if you imply that the person you are talking to is not, of course, in this category.

Sensible ministers speak at length only when they really need to, or when there are genuine points made in the debate that require an answer. Bridget Prentice, with whom I worked in the Justice Department, could knock off an SI in about fifteen minutes. In fact, we took to timing them to see how quickly we could finish one and it was much easier to get people to turn up for her committees as a result. Charles Clarke, having been confronted with a whole host of spurious points from the opposition, once stood up and announced that there had been no points of substance made in the debate and that he was not going to waste time replying. Of course, there are times when there are genuine debates to be had and good ministers and good whips recognise this and act accordingly, but you do not want ministers using up all the allotted time just for the sake of it and you should make that clear.

As you prowl the committee corridor, take a look at who is sitting outside the committees, either doing their own work or drinking coffee. As I said earlier, people do need breaks and some people will only turn up for committee if they can sit outside and wait for a vote while they get on with something else. Of course, they should be listening to the scintillating debate within and making up their mind about the issue but this counsel of perfection is seldom followed. You should be making sure that the coffee-drinkers have not strayed so far away from their committee that it would be difficult for them to get back in if a vote is called and you should ensure that there are not too many people being let out of the same committee. Giving people a break is sensible, but not having a majority there all the time is likely to lead to defeat. If you find that this is happening, you should ask why and, if some people are being particularly difficult with one of the whips, you need to gently encourage the whip not to put up with their nonsense any longer.

Above all, watch what is happening as you stroll about. Which of the new whips looks particularly nervous? Who has a grip on the job and who doesn't? Who is a soft touch for a sob story and who is favouring particular people by letting them be absent from committees? You should note all these things as you go around and then check the attendance registers afterwards. Each whip will have filled one in and you should ask why certain people are not there. If there is a good and reasonable explanation, then that's fine, but if people are being allowed not to attend because they have given some daft excuse, then you will need to have a word with the whip involved and tell them not to accept such excuses in future. Often, the people who are trying it on are ex-ministers who try to con new whips into believing that they have much more important things to do, or people who think that whatever meeting they had scheduled is more important than government business. It isn't, and you should make that clear. People who do not turn up at all without any explanation should be asked for one and then you should immediately place them on another committee, preferably the most boring one you can find to be held at the most inconvenient time. Remember that this is a war of attrition. They are going to give in before you do.

You will also find that you have other duties that go with your position, some official and some unofficial. As well as writing to the Queen, my official duties included taking messages to the palace and bringing messages from the Queen to the House. My unofficial duties included, I discovered, being a shoulder to cry on for new whips, as well as their back-up when their department was being difficult. I also became one of the people the whips' assistants passed on awkward callers to when they could not get rid of them.

Bringing the messages is the job most likely to expose you to ridicule. As a Vice-Chamberlain, you receive a wand of office upon appointment, which you have to collect from the Queen. It looks like a snooker cue because that is exactly what it is. When you leave office, it will be engraved with your name and returned to you but, in the meantime, it exists to provide a source of mirth for your friends when messages have to be delivered.

The first time I had to do this I looked up the procedure. I needed to go to the palace to collect the message first, which I did, wondering why it could not simply be put in the post. The instructions then told me that 'the Vice-Chamberlain appears at the bar of the House'. I imagined myself suddenly emerging from a puff of smoke. Sadly, there was no such luck.

The smoke might have provided cover for my humiliation, however. I had to walk forward six paces, bow, go forward another six paces and then read out the message before handing it to a clerk, all the time clutching my snooker cue in one hand. I managed this to the accompaniment of a barrage of comments from the benches below the gangway centring on whether I would be any use in a tournament, how well I had read etc. I then had to repeat the six paces and bowing routine but this time backwards. I had just about managed to keep a straight face through the first part of the process but, as I steadily progressed backwards, trying to keep in a straight line and not look like a drunk wobbling out at closing time, my face cracked. Under the relentless barrage, I gave in and laughed. Do not ever try to perform this process in high heels, whether male or female. You will wobble and make yourself look even more ridiculous than you do already. The only other piece of advice I have is that, if you are going to give two fingers your colleagues in revenge for their constant barrage of jokes, make sure that you are not on camera. I managed to duck out of the way, bob a half-curtsey and gesticulate at my friends without being caught. While this passes as a sign of affection in Parliament, it was only afterwards I realised what would have happened if I hadn't got out of the way of the cameras. It might have been the shortest stint as Vice-Chamberlain that anyone had ever had. Only stately baronesses of advanced years who have previously been secret agents and learnt to kill people can get away with such behaviour. It is unlikely that you will qualify for an exemption on any of these grounds.

I had broken the cardinal rule for any whip, but particularly for a senior one: always appear calm and in control, even if chaos is breaking out all around you. This is especially true for the unofficial duties you will have to perform. When some poor soul comes to you to confess that they have not found speakers for that day's business, or that their committee is not going to have a government majority that afternoon, you are not allowed to scream and call them an incompetent idiot, even if they are. They have come to you because they rely on you to be able to sort things out and because they are too afraid to tell the Deputy Chief Whip. So sort it out you will, by cajoling people, threatening them, blackmailing when necessary, until the committee has enough members and there are plenty of people willing to speak in the main debate. Then you will go and tell the Deputy Chief Whip anyway because he needs to know who is not pulling their weight and because you don't want to be the one accused of keeping things from him. Remember that Deputy Chief Whips (at least the one I worked with) are all-seeing and all-knowing and so he will find out anyway, but only tell him after you have put right the mistakes. After all, you don't want him to think you're incompetent as well. While doing all this, your stress levels will rocket but you must go around looking happy and confident. Whips always have everything under control.

You may also find yourself, as I did, in receipt of the awkward phone calls. Once again, you should remind yourself that this is not because of your marvellous ability to deal with difficult situations but because the whips' assistants are also scared of the Deputy and don't want to put the calls through to him. These phone calls will usually be from ministers asking if they can be spared the onerous task of coming in to vote, or from civil servants who believe that whatever meeting their minister is involved in at that particular time is far more important than maintaining the government's majority in Parliament. Only allow these requests if they are involved in something absolutely vital. Such occasions are very rare and you will know which ministers you can believe when they tell you this. You should never, ever believe the civil servants. To them, each meeting is more vital than the government winning a vote for the simple reason that they do not find themselves struggling to keep their job if the government is defeated. You, and their minister, will.

You will also find yourself acting as a back-up for other whips, who will pass phone calls on to you when they are getting nowhere or when a department is being particularly obstructive. Again, there is one rule you must abide by – never, ever undermine another whip, especially when dealing with a civil servant. If you do, all their authority in that department will vanish, civil servants will never take seriously anything they say and you will find yourself on the receiving end of frequent appeals against their rulings. You do not need this extra work so you should be as stern as possible with anyone who is giving a whip a hard time. In any case, everyone in the office stands or falls together. Do not listen to pleas about how difficult you are making life for a civil servant because you aren't and, even if you were, you shouldn't care. Your job is not to make their life easy, but to make sure the government wins votes. Do not believe any tales they tell you about how important it is for their minister to be elsewhere and never overrule another whip's decision, even if you believe they are wrong. You can tell them that afterwards but, as far as any government department is concerned, a whip's word has to be law. You, unfortunately, are going to be the hard-hearted bastard who won't listen and won't help them out. Unless the person you are speaking to is one of your constituents, which is very unlikely unless you are a London MP, you shouldn't care. It's part of your job.

Civil servants tend to be very repetitive and will keep you on the telephone for ages if you let them, so don't let them. Listen politely while they put their case, tell them no and if they start off again, just say that your decision is final and that you are not prepared to discuss it further. You should always give people a fair hearing before you turn them down, but it is to your advantage if they get the idea that you are not going to give in. Be firm if they persist. As I once asked a caller who would not give up, 'Which bit of the word "no" are you having a problem with?'. Not only did he not bother me again, but I clearly acquired a reputation as someone not to cross. I realised this when we were trying to reduce the number of SIs sent through by departments because they were becoming unmanageable and I heard someone else on the phone saying, 'Well, if you don't do it, I'll refer you to the whip in charge of SIs and she won't be happy.' It may not be better to be feared than loved in life generally, but it is a huge advantage if you are a government whip.

As well as cultivating an aura of general menace, you will need to learn to do without much sleep. This is not only because you work long hours, but because you can be contacted at any time. When someone has gone missing, or when there is a crisis, you can almost guarantee that your phone will ring just as you are nodding off to sleep. I have lost count of the number of times this happened to me. Sometimes there was an angry MP on the other end, only too eager to relate the details of the latest disloyal briefing that would appear in the press the next day (some people lead such sad lives they either stay up for the TV reviews of the following day's papers or get early editions). You cannot do anything about their complaint except listen and sympathise, and that is exactly what you should do. Ignore the impulse to ask them to ring back in the morning because someone ringing you at that time is loyal to the party. You need these people, especially when the going is rough, so telling them you have had a really bad day or that you are desperate to catch up on the sleep you have been missing all week is not going to work. They believe that you are paid to listen to what they are saying, and so you are. They may also be under the illusion that you can do something about it and you do not want to disabuse them of this idea. You are a whip and you need the illusion of power to do your job.

In times of real crisis, you will also get calls from other whips, including from the Chief. It is definitely not a good idea to ask him to call back. The reason he is ringing you is that he thinks you are reliable and capable of doing whatever he asks. You do not want him to get the idea that you are uninterested or useless, even if it is late at night. I was once woken by a call asking me to prevent someone going off abroad and missing an important vote because I was (wrongly) supposed to have had some influence on her. I felt dreadful. It was a Thursday night and I'd got home after having had little sleep all week. I was desperate to get my eight hours in before a busy day in the constituency. Yet I did it because I had to. There is no one else. The buck stops with you. You might ask yourself why this is so, because you are one of the most badly paid ministers in the government. The answer is the one that the sergeant gives to a panicky recruit in *Zulu* when he's asked 'Why us?' He says, 'Because we're here, lad. Ain't nobody else.'

These late-night calls are bad enough when you are on your own in a London flat. When you are at home, they are likely to disturb your family as well, so keep your mobile by your bedside and answer it quickly. At least you will only wake one other person (assuming your partner doesn't sleep like the dead) and you can creep downstairs to do any other calls that are needed. Calls coming through on the landline are likely to wake your kids. Unlike you, they will be excited because they believe that something important must be happening and you will have great difficulty getting them back to sleep. All of you will end up exhausted and fractious and you will feel even worse when you remember that there is no overtime pay or time off in lieu. You shouldn't have joined if you can't take the pressure. Politicians get no sympathy.

Chapter 18

Dealing with the royals

THERE WERE ONCE many fine customs associated with the government Whips' Office. Lord Commissioners of Her Majesty's Treasury used to act as intermediaries for distributing government money, receiving it in their own bank accounts. Whips used to receive a haunch of venison from the royal estates every Christmas. Sadly the first has long gone and Tony Blair, anxious to show he was leading a modern government, abolished the second owing to the difficulties of carrying a large piece of dead deer home on the West Coast Main Line. Despite frequent calls from government whips for these fine old traditions to be restored, largely driven by the thought

of how much overnight interest could be earned on the price
of an aircraft carrier and the rising cost of Christmas turkeys,
no Prime Minister has ever listened to these very reasonable
demands. That's because most Prime Ministers do not understand the value of their whips.

Instead, whips have been left with a few totally outdated
and useless customs that cause them a great deal of bother
and benefit no one. Most of these stem from the fact that senior whips hold titles in the royal household. The Deputy Chief
Whip is the Comptroller of the Household; the next in line
is the Treasurer and then, last, comes the Vice-Chamberlain.
The Chief Whip escapes this by virtue of both being a member of the Cabinet and having more important things to do.

The duties of the Comptroller and the Treasurer are limited
to riding in the carriage procession when the State Opening
of Parliament takes place and attending the royal garden parties held in London. If you ever watch the carriage procession
and wonder who those people you have never seen before
are, they are probably government whips. To enable them to
carry out these duties, they are allowed to purchase morning
suits, for which they can claim reimbursement. Since they will
never wear these on any other occasion and the 'perk' is tax-
able at 40 per cent, they are effectively paying for something
they don't want and will never use again (at least if they are
Labour whips).

The Vice-Chamberlain gets lumbered with even more royal
duties. In addition to writing to the Queen every day, taking
messages to the palace and attending garden parties, he or

she must act as the 'hostage' for the Queen's safe return when
she opens Parliament. The custom dates back to when rela-
tions between the monarch and Parliament were, to say the
least, not good.

If you have to carry out this duty, your first problem will
be deciding what to wear. As with many other things in life,
it is much easier if you're a man. Like the other senior whips,
you will be allowed to purchase a morning suit and you can
wear this both for your hostage duties and for garden parties.
Women will not find it so easy since the rules were drawn up
long before women held any of these positions and government bureaucracy does not understand that a woman cannot
wear the same outfit on four occasions in the same place, with
a lot of the same people. Try to find a nice suit or something
that you can wear to a wedding or a family christening afterwards and then at least it will not be wasted.

So, you will get dressed up and then you will try to sneak out
of the House of Commons without encountering any of your
colleagues. You will try, but will find it impossible. Just accept
that one of the reasons we still indulge in these daft rituals is to
give people a good laugh. Other MPs will see you and they will
make fun of you because it is your role on that day to contrib-
ute to the sum of human happiness by looking a prat. Garden
party days are better than the day of the State Opening simply
because, on the latter, it is almost mandatory for the whips to
appear in the tea room. There is a tradition that Labour whips
involved in the ceremony have their photograph taken with
the tea-room staff to the accompaniment of sarcastic whistles

and old jokes from their comrades. Try to bear this well, realising that you will have done it yourself in the past.

For the State Opening, your Deputy Chief Whip will demand that you leave early. The cars will arrive to collect you and, by hook or by crook, you will be in one. In the year when I was the hostage, my heel broke just as we left the tea room. I ran frantically back to my office in stocking feet to find a spare pair of shoes and then tried to make my way back down, only to find that, because I was not wearing a pass, I could not get through some doors. I found a circuitous route downstairs only to discover that the two other whips had gone, leaving me to follow in another car. Nothing will be allowed to delay a departure for the palace.

I set off, feeling uncomfortable in shoes that did not go with my outfit, only for the car to be stopped by a police officer as we tried to turn out of Parliament Square. Some patient explanation by the driver was needed to convince him that 'You can't go up there' did not apply to the Queen's hostage and that Her Majesty could not leave until I arrived. I was close to asking his name, on the grounds that it would be interesting to know who had delayed the entire State Opening, when he agreed to let us through. I arrived in plenty of time, ready to confront the flunkeys of Buck House.

You will have to realise when dealing with these people that they believe that you are the lowest form of life. They work for royalty so, however menial their job might be in reality, they will think themselves superior to you simply because you are not, and never will be, royalty. They are, generally, the most terrible snobs. So, as I followed the other two whips in, I announced that I was the hostage and asked where I should wait. They stuck me in a small room off the hall where I waited for some time while nothing happened. Finally, someone in what I presume was a footman's outfit appeared, although he looked as if he had escaped from a Ruritanian comedy. 'You must follow me immediately!' he commanded. At this point you should put your foot down. You are an elected Member of Parliament and not there for grumpy footmen to shout at because they are having a bad day, especially when it is their fault that you are not where you should be.

They will never admit that they have forgotten about you or put you in the wrong room, so imperious disdain is the best response. Like me, you will need to learn to 'do posh'. My friends tell me I'm very good at this so I looked down my nose, adopted my best convent-educated voice and enunciated clearly, 'Well, I have been waiting for some considerable time.' Such creatures will not, of course, deign to reply to you because you are beneath their notice but you will gain the satisfaction of having made it clear that you are not a person to be trifled with. You can then proceed at your own stately pace to wherever he wishes to lead you. He may try to hurry, but will have to keep looking back to see that he hasn't lost you and you won't want to arrive out of breath anymore than he will want to arrive without you, so don't worry. Just keep him in sight because the place is like a rabbit warren.

On State Opening day, you will find yourself in the hands of the Lord Chamberlain, with whom you will wait to see

HMQ off and in to the royal coach. Then you can watch the event on TV until the Queen returns. There will usually be a couple of young men around called Alexander, simply because most of the young men who work at the palace bear this suitably imperial name. I never learnt to sort out the Alexanders from one another but this needn't bother you too much. You are simply required to make polite conversation with them and with the Lord Chamberlain who, I found, was a cheerful and entertaining soul, even though I assumed that when he said that he lived in North Yorkshire that meant he owned half of it (at least!).

You will find that a similar process gets under way if you have to visit the Queen for any other reason, such as taking a message from the House. A slick operation ensures that you will be met by a lady-in-waiting and an equerry, who will entertain you until the sovereign is ready to see you.

On all these occasions you should steer clear of politics. Polite conversation about the weather, how the ceremony is proceeding, if it's State Opening, or how nice the ladies-in-waiting look is the order of the day. It will be hard-going because you have practically nothing in common with these people, but they are used to keeping conversations flowing. I did once meet an equerry who was interested in what whips do, but he was an exception. Do not allow yourself to think that these conversations matter, except as an opportunity for you to prove that all politicians are not complete oafs. These people are merely carrying out their duties and will move on to the next visitor as soon as you have left. However, it is not wise to tell them scurrilous stories about your colleagues, or to relate the latest parliamentary gossip or to comment in any way at all on what the government may be planning to do. It will, you can be sure, be passed on to people who you would rather did not know about it. No, your aim is to convince your listeners that you are an extremely dull person with nothing memorable to say at all. Count this as an achievement.

As I have said, you will also be forced to attend garden parties, again wearing formal dress. Your role on these occasions is to help 'marshal' the lines of people waiting to see either the Queen or the Duke of Edinburgh. There is a line for each of them and you will be expected to help find people to whom they can be introduced. Do not think that you can pick out at random anyone who looks vaguely interesting or eager. In fact, it's wise to leave the choice entirely to the Deputy Chief Whip. The reason is simple. Lots of staff from the House of Commons attend the garden parties and all of them hope that you will get them introduced to the Queen. Picking a way through this without causing grave offence to the people left out is a delicate art, best left to someone above your pay grade. After all, these people prepare your food and clean your office, serve you your tea and coffee. I am not for one moment suggesting that anything dodgy might make its way into the next week's curry, but people lose all sense of reason when the monarch is around, so you never know. It's always best to be able to say that it was nothing to do with you.

People love garden parties. They adore being invited onto the lawns of Buck House and then eating their sandwiches and strawberries feet away from the Queen. For many people, it is the highlight of their lives. It will not be so for you. You will be walking up and down, trying to look interested, making small talk with the crowd to avoid looking superior. Your feet will ache because you have had to get there well in advance. No one knows or cares who you are and you have a pile of work waiting for you back in the office. Do not go as far as one whip who asked a curly-headed lady if she had come far, proximity to the royals clearly beginning to change her speaking patterns.

'I'm Rebekah Wade,' said the editor of the *News of the World*, as she was then.

'Oh yes,' said this whip, who clearly did not spend time perusing the tabloids, 'but have you come far?'

Do not believe that you can escape early from any of this. You will not be allowed to leave until the Queen leaves. Then you can let other people enjoy themselves without you and rush back to your real job. On one occasion, no car had turned up to collect us and we were expecting an early vote. We ran down Birdcage Walk, tailcoats flapping and my high heels clicking on the pavement so we could make it in time to change back into our normal outfits before having to appear in the lobby. The thought of missing the vote was bad, but the thought of having to appear in all our finery was worse. I always felt rather sorry for the driver who hadn't turned up as instructed. The Deputy Chief Whip wanted an explanation for his absence.

Chapter 19

The Prime Minister

THE PRIME MINISTER is your boss, but he is a boss you will hardly ever see, and then usually only when things have gone wrong. This is true for most government ministers, other than the big beasts of the Cabinet, but it makes life especially difficult for whips, who are supposed to be the enforcers of the prime ministerial will. You are one of the 'Prime Minister's whips', which is why there is now a tradition of every Whips' Office having its photo taken with the Prime Minister. You are part of a team intended to deliver what he requires to be delivered. Those who have never had to do the job believe that a winning majority can be conjured from thin air to suit anyone's whim.

You know that isn't true but, fortunately, it is not your duty to say so. That is what the Chief Whip is paid for and why he earns more than you do. If it is your job to sometimes tell the Prime Minister that something cannot be done, the very least you deserve is a decent salary and a good pension package.

I was never sure why Gordon Brown decided to put me in the Whips' Office after so many years on the back benches. A kind view would be that someone recommended me to him. An unkind view might say that he was desperate. Still, he took a chance with me and I have always been grateful to him. The press reported that a 'team of Brownite enforcers' had been sent to the Whips' Office, the inference being, as someone once put it to me, that we were 'a bunch of thugs'. No doubt this was intended to be hurtful, but whips take such comments as a compliment.

Once appointed, you will hardly ever see the Prime Minister, except for the obligatory photo. You will, however, frequently be told what he wants, or is supposed to want. 'The PM wants' or 'No. 10 wants' are phrases that will be trotted out to you time and time again, either by ministers who are trying to tell you why some totally mad policy they have come up with has to be forced through the PLP, or by some very junior Spad trying to throw his weight about and to prove he knows more than you do. Ignore them all. The only reliable guide to what the Prime Minister wants is the Chief Whip. He sits in Cabinet, he is the person involved in all the discussions about what is and what is not achievable, and he is the one tasked with telling the Prime Minister what can and cannot be done. No one else is worth listening to.

The Chief is like Moses going up the mountain to bring down the law. You may argue about it, but once the decision is made you will have to enforce it. That's what you get paid for.

Ministers will try to use the Prime Minister like a human shield, usually as an excuse for not being where you need them to be. They will tell you that they have a very important meeting in No. 10 (it's usually with a spotty youth who looks like he's popped in to do the photocopying), or that they are helping to write a prime ministerial speech, or that they are far too busy drafting policy to attend to the business of legislating. Don't believe it. If the Prime Minister really needs to see someone, his office will be able to confirm this for you. Mostly, people are either being lazy or want to seem much closer to the centre of power than they really are. This pretence may help them but it doesn't need to bother you too much.

One minister, who was very resentful about having to serve on a committee, bombarded me with phone calls telling me of all the important things he had to do for the Prime Minister and why I was wasting his time simply trying to get a government Bill on the statute book. Eventually, he rang the Prime Minister himself to complain and was told to get back on the committee. Loyalty cuts both ways and it's nice to work for a Prime Minister who backs up his whips.

So, while your day-to-day contact with the Prime Minister is limited, you will encounter him on two separate kinds of occasion. The first is when the whips have just won a tight vote. It is often the case that the Prime Minister will appear in the office to thank his whips, and so he should. On a couple of occasions, after these death-defying feats of escapism, we were all invited over to Downing Street where there was a reception going on. We went, of course. One of the unwritten rules of the Whips' Office is that you never refuse a free drink. I often wonder what other guests thought of the arrival of a sweaty, exhausted-looking troupe of people who proceeded to grab glasses of wine, swoop hungrily on the trays of nibbles provided and then simply talk among themselves in a corner, keeping an eye out for more passing waiters who they could relieve of their burdens. They probably thought we were some deserving charity cases invited to show how inclusive the government really was.

Gordon was good at acknowledging the work of his whips, either by taking us over to drink lots of wine while he wandered the room with only a glass of water, or in other ways. He gave each one of us an inscribed copy of Barack Obama's inaugural address, sent over without ceremony, simply as an acknowledgement of our sustained efforts. Such things are nice to have but we did not, of course, have time to read it. By then we were too busy trying to keep the government on the road.

You will also see the Prime Minister when you manage to lose a vote or, more likely, you will feel him looming around like a dark cloud waiting for an explanation of the incompetence of the people he has appointed. It will not, of course, be the fault of the whips. When votes are won, it is because of the slick operation run by the Whips' Office. When they are lost, it is down to an incompetent minister who has either put forward legislation that cannot win support or failed to win people over to his side.

When we lost a vote on the Gurkhas' right to settle in the UK, I had been uneasy all afternoon, telling people that it just didn't 'feel right'. I kept being told that everything was under control. After all, it was simply an opposition day motion, and how many of our people would vote with the Tories? The answer was 'enough of them'. As the vote was announced, I saw Gordon heading to his office and his PPS materialised at my elbow asking me to tell the Chief Whip to come and see him. I stealthily made my way along the second row of benches, trying not to look too obvious and leaned forward, hand over my mouth so that no one opposite could make out what I was saying. 'The Prime Minister would like to see you.'

'I'm sure he would,' came the reply with a sigh.

After a defeat, people gather in the office like mourners at a funeral. There is no point in you saying that you saw it coming, even if you did. Your colleagues will not thank you and, in any case, any failure is a collective failure. People will all chew over the reason everything went wrong, cursing people who just give in to pressure groups, discussing what punishments are suitable for those who hand the opposition a victory. It relieves everyone's feelings, but it won't change the result. Like football managers, you should be planning for the next game, which, in this case, was how to support the poor unfortunate minister who was going to have to come to the House and make a humiliating climb-down. Also, again like football managers, you will be hoping that the chairman doesn't decide to sack you after just one defeat and that the Chief does not emerge from the Prime Minister's office saying either that he has tendered your collective resignation or that you have all been sacked. Fortunately for us, Gordon was more forbearing than the media liked to suggest. The Chief emerged weary but intact and we stayed on to fight another day. Either Prime Ministers have to learn to live with the unexpected, just like the rest of us, or he had been convinced by Nick's explanation that there was no way we could have seen it coming.

Whatever happens, in victory or defeat, your job is to support the Prime Minister. You may say, in the privacy of the Whips' Office, that he is asking the impossible. You may tell the Chief that what is being asked of you is just not deliverable. Then you will go out and try to deliver it anyway. It is the Chief's job to try to persuade a Prime Minister that something is wrong or can't be done but, once a decision is made, you will go out and find the votes to support it. That is what being a whip means. Loyalty comes first, whatever happens. If you can't manage that, then you're in the wrong place.

Chapter 20

Dealing with other parties

TERRIBLE THOUGH THIS is or may seem, an unavoidable part of being a whip involves actually talking to your opponents. You have to organise the business, so it is helpful for you to know something about what the opposition are planning. It helps if your opposite number in the opposition Whips' Office is a decent sort who will be honest with you about what is going on, but you aren't likely to find such a paragon. He's a whip, like you, the only difference being that your job is to get the government's business through and his job is to try to defeat it. He will pull any stunt to achieve this because he wants to make his mark and be promoted. Like a mafia hit, it's nothing personal, just business.

You will find it much easier to deal with your opponents if you recognise this from the start. You can't expect any favours. If you make a mistake, then they will use it against you. So not reading the Order Paper properly or a failure to understand when the votes will come will be seized upon and you will suffer for it. In the same way, if you don't make sure you have a majority on a committee, it is unreasonable to expect the opposition whip to shrug his shoulders and say, 'Ah, well, we're not going to call any votes.' It's not his job to save your skin.

However, while an opposition whip can capitalise on your failings, he should never lie to you and you should not lie to him. This doesn't mean that you can expect him to tell you the whole truth any more than you will tell him everything. It simply means that he should not tell an outright lie. There is some honour among whips. There has to be or the House of Commons could not function. So, if he tells you that his side are not going to vote on a particular issue, you should be able to believe him, although it's always wise to double check. Unfortunately, such a clear statement is very rare. It is far more likely that he will tell you he doesn't know or that no decision has yet been made. This may even be true, on rare occasions, but it usually means that he is simply not going to tell you and you will have to keep the massed ranks of the parliamentary party hanging around just in case there is a vote. It will happen because about the only power the opposition has is to make the life of the governing party miserable by keeping all its MPs hanging about while they send half their troops home. When no vote is called, your own side will swear and call you incompetent. This is not pleasant but it is better than the alternative of explaining to the Prime Minister, or, even worse, to the Chief Whip, exactly why you have just presided over the defeat of a piece of government legislation.

If any opposition whip does break his word to you, immediate action is called for. Tell your Chief or the Deputy immediately and they will then ensure that they use whatever means they can to make the opposition's life as difficult as possible. Unfortunately, this is harder than them making your life a misery, but it can be done. A refusal to pair works when you have a big majority, but not otherwise, as there will be people on your own side who need to be elsewhere and you will not be able to let them go. However, not giving the opposition notice of the business until the last possible moment or scheduling opposition days at the worst possible time for them are always tactics worth considering. If you really want to get your own back then it's a good idea to put on voteable business to coincide with events that their members will be desperate to attend – as a Labour whip, this would mean scheduling around Royal Ascot or the day of a major Tory fundraising event like the black and white ball. Conservative whips may like to find out the dates of union conferences. Really serious retaliation can ensue if you know the date of the opposition's whips' dinner and can schedule votes to coincide with that. However, you should always remember that what you do to people when they are in opposition can be done to you when they are in government, so you should think carefully. It's always possible, of course, that a junior whip has not told the truth because he thinks it's clever rather than on the instructions of anyone above him in the hierarchy. In such cases you can rest assured that the bollocking he will get from his own Chief, after, of course, your boss has let him know what retaliation is coming his way, will be far worse than anything you could do. It is possible to try to be too clever and new and inexperienced whips will sometimes try it. Once they have heard from their own Chief Whip, they are unlikely to make the same mistake again.

You may be worrying about what you do with the other opposition parties, to which the answer is 'not much'. I once astonished a civil servant who was preparing for a Bill by telling her that I wasn't interested in what the Liberal Democrats thought about it or what amendments they might move. This is the same view that the government took after 2010, even though they were supposed to be partners. She looked down mournfully at her carefully prepared notes and indicated that she was astonished by this dismissive attitude, but it was based on simple arithmetic: they didn't have the numbers to be a threat to us, so I didn't care. The same is true of other minor parties. The only time that you need to even think about them is when a big rebellion is threatened and they are going to vote with your rebels and the opposition. Even then, there is not much you can do about it. The Scottish and Welsh Nationalists are blood enemies of the Labour Party and will do anything to make them look bad. If you are a Tory whip, they hate your party just as much. There is nothing you can offer them since they seek to displace Labour in their own areas, so concentrate on getting your own side in to vote.

There is one minor party for which you can make an exception and, surprisingly, it is the Democratic Unionist Party (DUP). When your own side are rebelling against an anti-terrorism measure or refusing to support the latest clampdown on criminals, it is usually possible to get the DUP to vote with you. Indeed, where anti-terrorism measures are concerned, they do not generally need any persuasion. On other occasions they will extract a price, which is why Belfast has two good airports and Northern Ireland as a whole has excellent motorways, power stations and roads. All sorts of infrastructure projects, which are the envy of many MPs, have been built in Northern Ireland by governments anxious to maintain the good will of Ulster Unionists. The exact negotiations, which, of course, have never taken place, will be done far above your pay grade. Your job is to make sure that a friendly atmosphere is maintained.

This is surprisingly easy if you don't talk about politics. Generally, when they are not shouting from platforms or waving banners, unionists are polite and well-mannered, especially towards women. If you stick to topics like the weather, how well the latest VIP visit went or the tourist attractions of the province, you will be fine. Advanced tuition in why you should not say Derry, instead of Londonderry, or refer to how well the Pope's visit went, can be provided by your Northern Ireland ministers. Similarly, you should not point out that your family came from Mayo or you had a relative killed in the Easter Rising, even if it's true (and many Labour MPs do have Irish blood). I always found it easier because my surname was Welsh and so my Irish ancestry went unnoticed.

You should also take time to be nice to the staff in the DUP office, not only because they are pleasant people and deserve your courtesy, but because they will be able to tell you where their MPs are and help you when you need to get them into Parliament. It's a sad fact that Northern Ireland MPs are not seen in the House of Commons frequently. They come for Prime Minister's Questions and turn out in force for Northern Ireland questions but, at other times, they are thin on the ground. It makes it all the more important that you take the opportunity to be nice to them when they are around.

If you do have to adopt this strategy, you may find it wise not to listen to their speeches much. There are two reasons for this. One is that no Ulster Unionist has ever made a short speech. In fact, no one from Northern Ireland has ever made a short speech. The other is that, when speaking, most of them turn from nice, polite people into something approaching a polar bear with a grievance. Listening to them will only send your blood pressure up and make you want to reply. Just be thankful that you are a whip and that you deal with process rather than policy.

The SDLP are, of course, on your side if you are a Labour whip. They are members of a sister party and will usually support you in the lobbies unless there is a particular reason relating to Northern Ireland for them not to do so. If that is the case, you will not shift them because they value their seats more than your approval and you will not be able to talk them out of this very sensible view. Your task will be to ensure that they turn up when you need them there and so you should make sure that you spend time getting to know them. Remember that these are people under pressure. They are decent souls who are being squeezed by Unionists on the one side and Sinn Féin on the other while generally trying to do a good job for their communities and steer them away from violence. They have seen their party become more and more marginalised despite the fact that they were in the vanguard fighting for civil rights in Northern Ireland. Imagine how you would feel in their situation and be nice. You may learn something from them.

When you are finding all this niceness wearing and feeling that it goes against your nature as a whip, just remember that there may come a time when it will save your government from defeat. Listening to someone's grievances and offering a few kind words is not much to ask to save you from that, is it? Think of it as a way of becoming a nicer, more enlightened person in preparation for the time you leave the Whips' Office, as you surely will eventually. If that doesn't work, think how you might feel if you lose a vote and someone tells the Chief that they didn't turn out to support it because you were not interested in talking to them. If that doesn't convince you that playing nice is sometimes the best strategy, then nothing will. This advice does not, of course, apply to dealing with the Liberal Democrats, who are the most untrustworthy party in the House and entirely consistent. They will always bite the hand that feeds them. If you need an outlet for your mean and nasty side, practise on them. Your own side will love it, as will the Tories, even if they pretend not to.

Chapter 21

How to leave

I T WAS ENOCH Powell who said that all political careers end in failure and this has been quoted ever since in order to suggest to politicians that nothing they do really matters. It's not, however, the best way to think about your life. Some things you do will matter, especially in the Whips' Office. Keeping the government on the road, saving your colleagues from abject humiliation, or at least supporting them when that humiliation occurs – these actions do make a real difference to people's lives.

What you really do have to remember is another, much truer phrase: 'All government jobs are temporary.' Whether you lose your job because your party gets thrown out in a general election or because the Prime Minister decides it's time for a reshuffle, sooner or later you will have to go. The only way of leaving that gets you any plaudits is dying, but this is a rather extreme course to take to avoid being sacked and you should remember that, after the minute's silence you will be accorded by the PLP, they will be wondering who will get your seat.

Dying in office does make you worth far more to your family than living on to collect your pension (a fact that you should make every effort to conceal from them, by the way) but it has very unpleasant side effects. In any event, the electorate will only just about forgive death as the cause of a by-election if it is through no fault of your own and you won't want to be remembered as the person who caused the loss of a seat.

It's much better to accept that one day you will have to go – with a pulse. This is a hard process for anyone, but it is particularly true for a whip because your team works so closely together. Being cast out from the Whips' Office is like being thrown out of your own home and it is very hard for people to adjust to the outside world where they don't have friends sitting next to them with whom they can share their frustrations and where they don't know what's going on before most other people do.

For this reason, you should be preparing your exit from the moment you are appointed. Some will be young enough to go on to be ministers or shadow ministers. These former whips may well be moved to other jobs by the Prime Minister after they have served a period in the office. Think carefully before you decide whether this is the route for you. The life of a Parliamentary Under-Secretary for widgets is often nasty, brutish and short and involves being given all the late-night Adjournment Debates and other work that those above you don't want to do. Most people only accept the job because they believe it will lead to higher things. Assess the prospects of such a move carefully and if you don't think you have a chance of further promotion, think about going to the back benches instead.

Most people, however, will not get the choice. They will be sacked either by the Prime Minister or by the electorate. It used to be said in the House that 'you don't sack whips'. Instead, they were moved to other jobs for a year or two and then sacked. Tony Blair abandoned this very sensible convention and his attitude has been followed by the current Prime Minister. (Note to future Prime Ministers: putting a lot of people who know how the House is organised and where all the bodies are buried, and who have the capacity to cause major problems for the running of your business, on the back benches is probably not the smartest move you will ever make.) If this happens to you, remember the mantra 'modesty on appointment and graciousness when sacked'. People will be far more sympathetic towards you if you do not go around venting all your grievances. Keep them for when you are at home. Above all, it is not advisable to make them to the Prime Minister himself. One minister responded with some choice language to news of his sacking, given to him by phone, only to hear his wife shout, 'That's the fucking Prime Minister you're talking to!' Save it for later. You're entitled to a day or two feeling hard-done-by, but that's all. After all, you are still an MP, you still have a job and you are far better off than most people in this world.

When you have allowed yourself to feel miserable for a couple of days, then stop. Get your hair done and buy a new outfit, if you're female. It's important not to look down and dowdy. Get yourself a new suit if you're a man. Then get back into the House of Commons and start speaking. Ask questions, find a new cause to pursue. There are plenty of wrongs out there that need righting. Whatever you do, do not allow yourself to hide away feeling miserable.

Getting back into the chamber is especially difficult for ex-whips who may not have spoken for years, except to say 'I beg to move' and 'Tomorrow', which hardly count as speeches to set the world on fire. The one advantage you have is that some colleagues will have forgotten that you are capable of making a speech and newer members will not have heard you speak at all. So get in there and get on with it. They will be astonished that you can actually perform in the chamber and the longer you leave it, the more difficult it will get. Treat it as if you have fallen off a bike and know that you just have to get back on.

You will suddenly find yourself with more time on your hands than you have had for years and it will take you time to adjust. No longer do you need to be in early in the morning and your days will not be so frantic any more. Believe me, it will take you at least a year to adjust properly to this because you have become used to living on adrenalin. You may look forward to sleeping in later in the mornings, but you will wake up at your usual time. You will wonder whether there is something you should be doing and realise that there isn't. So think of all the things that you promised yourself you would do if only you had the time, and start doing them. Reintroduce yourself to your family and give them an up-to-date picture. They probably just about remember you. Take them out somewhere nice, visit those museums and galleries in London that you always promised yourself you would go and see one day. At home, tackle some of the jobs you've been putting off because you were so busy. It doesn't matter much what you do as long as you do something.

Above all, resist the temptation to tell people that you are hard-done-by. You may have lost your ministerial post, or been moved to a portfolio that you don't much like, but no one will either understand or sympathise. The reason is clear but brutal. You still have a job; you are better paid than most of the population. You are incomparably more privileged than most of the people in this world, so don't whine.

In Parliament, you can rediscover the pleasure of spending some time with your friends, assuming that you have taken the advice in this book and still have friends. It's likely that some of them will have lost their jobs too. Others who have never been in government will welcome you back to the back benches. You can linger in the tea room when you are genuinely not working, you will be able to eat in the dining room without watching the clock and wondering when a division will be called or whether the bench whip really is keeping a proper eye on the business. There are lots of compensations available to you in your situation.

You will also have a lot to offer to anyone who wants to pursue an issue in Parliament when you decide what your cause should be. Lots of information from charities and campaigns comes across MPs' desks and, now you are no longer a whip, you may even have time to read it. This will help you find issues you want to get involved with. Take your time about choosing what to become involved in and avoid the temptation to jump into the first thing that you see just because you are desperate for something to do. Choose an issue that you really have an interest in either because there are links with your own personal experience, or because you have come across the problems in your own constituency, and then use the knowledge you have gained to help your chosen cause. After all, you have been a whip, you know how the House of Commons works. It's time to put that knowledge to good use.

For those facing a general election that they know is lost, the situation is rather different. You may hope that you are well-prepared for the loss of your seat, but rejection by the electorate is a particularly personal humiliation. You will need to stand next to your opponents and hear the cheers of other political parties as you are summarily thrown out. Those who really know that they are going to lose clear their offices out before the election so that they do not have to face returning to the House after a defeat. Others may be taken by surprise and find themselves suddenly having to come back to London and move out. If this happens to you, do it quickly and get it over with. The House of Commons is like a peculiar club and, once you have lost your membership, nothing is quite the same. People you meet will be nice to you, but face up to the fact that they are embarrassed and don't quite know what to say. It's the political version of survivors' guilt. They made it and you didn't and there may be no logical reason why. Keep in mind that luck plays a big role in any politician's success or failure.

You will also find that the casualties of war are not treated well by the House of Commons authorities. Once upon a time, you could go anywhere in the building and do what you liked. Now they will restrict your movements and want you out as quickly as possible. They need your office for a new member. You knew it was a brutal profession when you joined, but you are now finding out what that really means. Don't hang about. Clear your stuff out and get back home where you have other things to think about.

First, you will need to clear out your constituency office, deal with the confidential material you have there and, most importantly, arrange redundancy payments for your staff. There is plenty of advice available on all these things, but your staff should be the first priority. After all, they have served you loyally so you should do what you can to help them find another job. There may be new MPs in your own party looking for staff, although it is much easier for staff based in London to transfer. If you are lucky, there may be a newcomer in a nearby constituency who might take them on. Help them in any way you can. They're facing the same problems as you are.

Unless you are old enough to retire, you will then be faced with the uphill task of finding a job. Few MPs can just pick up the pieces where they left off. The jobs they used to do have changed beyond recognition and their career path has disappeared. Tories can usually get jobs with their friends in the City but, for Labour MPs, the situation is much harder. If you have lost your seat and your party is still in government, you will get approaches from all kinds of people, especially lobbyists. Remember they don't want you for your charm, good looks and extensive knowledge of the legislative process: they want you for who you know. The need to earn a living may drive you to look longingly upon such offers, but do some checking first. Talk to people who have lost their seats in the past and, if possible, those who have worked for that particular firm, and think carefully about whether you want to be back in the Westminster bubble now you are no longer an MP. There is no sadder sight than former MPs hanging around trying to drum up business for their new masters. Ask yourself whether you really want to be travelling down to London each week and what your prospects are in your own region. You may get paid less but have a better quality of life. On the other hand, you might have represented an area where there is no chance of getting another job and you will be forced to accept whatever is on offer. Don't, whatever you do, see this as a way back into Parliament or believe that your colleagues will treat you as if you are one of them. They won't because you aren't and, sooner or later, you will have to face up to it.

Still, wherever you go and whatever you do, you will always have your time in the Whips' Office to look back on. You did what most people never do. You became a Member of Parliament and a government minister. Others may have looked down on or despised the work you did, but you will know how essential it was. You have been in the engine room of politics – dirty, noisy and unpleasant it may be, but nothing moves without it. Cherish the experience and use it, but accept that it is time to move on. It was a big part of your life. Now, it will only be a fond memory. Only you will know how often you and your colleagues saved the government and what you had to do to achieve that. You will not appear in anyone's memoirs unless they choose to be dismissive or to despise you. You should be proud of that, for a good whip should never appear in print. You will know more about what really happened than the authors of those large, self-serving tomes. Whips always know more than they say, for that is how they deliver.

Keep that thought close and enjoy what comes after.

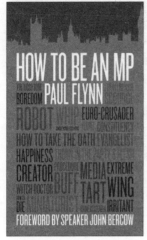
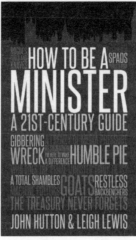